HOW TO READ THE BIBLE

THE MACMILLAN COMPANY
NEW YORK · CHICAGO
DALLAS · ATLANTA · SAN FRANCISCO
LONDON · MANILA

IN CANADA
BRETT-MACMILLAN LTD.
GALT, ONTARIO

HOW TO READ THE BIBLE

JULIAN PRICE LOVE

Revised Edition

New York · THE MACMILLAN COMPANY · 1959

Second Printing, 1963

Library of Congress catalog card number: 58-13177

Scripture quotations are from the Revised Standard Version of
the Bible, copyright 1946 and 1952 by the Division of Christian
Education of the National Council of the Churches of Christ
in the United States of America.

The Macmillan Company, New York
Brett-Macmillan Ltd., Galt, Ontario

Printed in the United States of America

To the memory of my Father
whose lengthy quotations from the Bible
are among my boyhood recollections
of delight and awe

BY WAY OF PREFACE

The occasion for this book is a series of convictions, many of them obvious, but some of them striking and compelling. Although the Bible is the world's most renowned book of religion, its faith is taught informally in relation to national and individual experiences. Though it contains a wide variety of theological thought and of literary styles of expression, its marvelously unified message has worldwide appeal. In spite of its orientalisms of dress and its setting in the experience of a small and strangely isolated people, it penetrates so clearly to the center of human need that it is readily understood and appreciated anywhere. The periodic cry of the peoples' lack of interest in the Bible is due to a misunderstanding of what its purpose is and to the awkward and uninviting way in which the English versions of the past have so often reached the public. It is surprisingly true that only a few simple helps are needed for the reading of the Bible so as to release its delights to many who think they cannot follow it.

The plan of these pages is, in general, threefold. The first six chapters illustrate a number of ways of becoming acquainted with the Bible. They should be followed consecutively. Chapters 7 and 8 are elaborations of what seem to be the best reading units for each book of the Bible. These do not make good consecutive reading, but are intended rather for reference. They are, however, the meat of the book, as they carry out its chief insistence, that the Bible ought to be read by "units of thought." The last four chapters deal with available helps toward reading and understanding the Bible, and are more truly separate chapters than the first six.

In the preparation of the first edition of this book, it was a joy to acknowledge the assistance given by many friends and colleagues at the Louisville Presbyterian Theological Seminary who read the pages in manuscript form; among them, President and Mrs. Frank H. Caldwell, Dr. and Mrs. Lewis J. Sherrill, Dr. W. D. Chamberlain, and Mrs. Emmett F. Horine. In appreciation of many requests for a second edition that should seek to bring the work up to date, I have been aided chiefly by the wise and faithful counsel of my wife, who has gone carefully over each sentence with me in an effort to improve both thought and style. Thanks are also due to Mr. Ernest M. White, librarian of the seminary, for his help with the bibliography.

Julian Price Love

CONTENTS

ix

HOW TO READ THE BIBLE

Chapter 1

CONTRASTING PICTURES

Some years ago it was my privilege to preach the centennial sermon for a Midwestern church. Arriving on the field Saturday evening, and having a few hours to spend in the pastor's library, I came upon the diary of the founder of the church. This volume, small and musty and well yellowed with age, gripped the imagination from the start. In it the veteran missionary of a hundred years before had poured out his heart over the trying problems of "this western wilderness." Such difficulties as the lack of preachers for the new churches that were rising, roads that made impossible the getting together of the woods dwellers, and the continual discovery of ignorance and superstition fill its pages. But no want is oftener bemoaned than the dearth of copies of the scriptures, or even of portions of them, and no words in the diary are more plaintive in their pathetic jubilation than the sudden outburst at the end of one weary record, "We stopped at noon, at a decent cabin, and found they had a Bible." Writing of others who did not possess this much, he says, "O how much they need to be looked up, by missionaries, and supplied with Bibles."*

That such words could be penned less than a century and a half ago in the midst of what is today a teeming populace well supplied with religious advantages!

It is hard for us who can buy one almost anywhere for a few cents to realize how recently Bibles were scarce and expensive. The tales of hunger for copies of "The Word" have too frequently taken to

* From *The Christian Traveller* by Isaac Reed, published 1826.

1

themselves the vistas of great distance and the glamor of other days. We remember the stories of the English Bible in the fourteenth century when John Wycliffe defied many leaders of the church in order to give the people the first complete Bible in their own tongue. Then a large amount of money was paid for a few sheets of the book, and records exist of a load of hay being given in exchange for the privilege of reading it for a day. Or we recall the Welsh tales of little Mary Jones who walked for days over the mountains to beg a Bible for herself, or the stories of the Englishmen who eagerly watched the shipping of goods from the Continent to find copies of Tyndale's translation smuggled in bales of hay or drygoods. But for many years the circulation of the Bible in the United States was also quite limited. Acquaintance with so much as its appearance was rare in some quarters, and the poor simply could not afford to buy a copy even when it was available.

A Modern Miracle

How completely all this has been changed is seen in the tremendous output of Bibles in the nineteenth and twentieth centuries. The American Bible Society, organized only a few years before the missionary wrote his diary, has exceeded the wildest dreams in the steadiness and growth of its work. In the first 140 years of its existence it published 44,000,000 copies of the complete Bible, and ten times that many New Testaments, in addition to many shorter portions of the scriptures. This work was done in some 350 languages and dialects. And Bible societies in other nations of the world have been very active too. Altogether the entire Bible is now available in some 180 different languages and dialects, and portions of it in more than 1,100. Truly, we may give thanks! The years that have passed since the good missionary penned his ardent cry in the American woods have seen a transformation in the distribution of the Bible to the people that far surpasses the most romantic story of the progress of science. When the Revised Standard Version was placed on the

American market in so dramatic a fashion in the fall of 1952, its first edition was already sold out!

Nor has this remarkable story been a tale of curiosity alone or of the seeking for security. True enough, there have been formal and perfunctory uses of the Bible, and there have been superstitious feelings that it was a good book to have around. But though the earlier period of family devotional reading was followed by a long era of neglect on the part of many, that has in turn been succeeded by a genuine revival of interest in the Book of books, its stories, its teaching, its theology. In family circles, on college campuses, in church school adult classes, it has become increasingly evident that men and women want to know what the Bible has to say and why it has so long held sway as the guide to men's faith.

Such a renewed interest has been aided by many fortunate circumstances. The twentieth century has witnessed a number of translations of the Bible into language that is much nearer daily speech and reading than that of the King James Version. Some of these translations are, indeed, quite free. The older works of such men as Weymouth, Moffatt, and Smith and Goodspeed prepared the way for more recent and still more popular renderings, such as that of Phillips. But the more exact versions, while all of them are but revisions of the King James, have gained a weight of authority that commands attention and respect even from those who do not make much use of them. Especially is this true of the Revised Standard Version, given to the American public by an interdenominational committee of thirty-two scholars, who whetted the appetites of Christians by publishing the New Testament in 1946, and then gave the entire Bible to the public six years later. Since then there has been a phenomenal growth in the number of those who talk about the Bible, and certainly to some degree of those who are actually reading it. Not only is the Revised Standard Version based on better manuscripts of the original Greek and Hebrew, but it is a translation into the language of today—not street language, but good current English—just as the King James was translated into the best English of its day. Paragraphs, the use of quotation marks, and especially the printing of poetry in poetical form, render this translation the best we can use if we really want to learn to know our Bibles. In this book all quotations are from the RSV, and all Biblical references are made to it. The publication of many guidebooks to study of the Bible, of many new commentaries on the Bible, some of them at least slanted in the direction of the layman, and of Bible dictionaries and atlases, has also contributed very really to the increased acclaim for the Bible. The fact that many denominations have published books of daily devotion in which passages of scripture have played a vital part has certainly served to set the Bible before many church families in a form in which they feel equal to handling it.

As humanity enters the "space age," facing as great transformations as those who first crossed the Atlantic or those who first flew in the air above it, man is growing increasingly conscious of his need for a spiritual guide which has not only proved serviceable to the pioneer but has outlasted the changeful arts of man's concocting. The need of a new sense of security in uncharted ways combines with the new means at the disposal of men to make the Bible a fresh and charming book to read and understand.

When the Protestant Bible Remains Closed

Yet, in spite of these favorable omens, there is still much evidence that the Bible is more admired than understood, more handled than used. Perhaps there are two main reasons why it is still a closed book to so many.

For one thing many people do not grasp what the Bible really is. They think of it as a kind of mystery to be fathomed only by highly trained intellects. Or they imagine it an arsenal of proof texts to demonstrate some theory of life. Or they go to it in search of rules whereby their life can be laid out for them, so many pointers to be gained that will make morality sure. People often approach the reading of the Bible from a sense of duty, scarcely realizing that it was meant to afford them the highest joy.

Let us be clear as to what the Bible actually is. It is the story of God's dealings with people, not primarily of his concern with the universe. It is the assurance that men need only one God and that they have at the very point of their need the kind of God who meets the human situation perfectly. For many people God is a problem to be discussed, but for the Bible man is the problem and God is the answer. The Bible takes God for granted; it never seeks to prove either his existence or his reality. It is concerned with demonstrating his nature and with wooing men to be his servants.

The Bible, then, presents the story of God's dealing with people —his making of humanity finite and yet in the image of the freedom of the infinite. Truly breathtaking is the assurance that God made man for perfect freedom and that he will be restless until he finds that freedom in yielding himself willingly to the very God who made him. God has chosen men; men did not first choose God. It is in one sense the whole of mankind that God has chosen, yet it has always been through a particular people that he has especially made clear his choice. These people have never been selected for their own greatness, but because God could use them as "Exhibit A" of his grace and mercy. In the Old Testament the people so chosen were the Jewish nation, in the New Testament the Christian church. Both nation and church find the fulfillment of their choice only by carrying out its purpose, that of making the love and truth of God known wherever they come into contact with humanity. Whenever the Hebrew of the old order or the church of the new tries to keep for selfish use the choice of God, it paradoxically loses that choice. The blessings of God will flow in only when they can flow through. The covenant of God has been made with his chosen people only so that they may be in a position to win all men to a covenant relation with God. The Bible in many scenes paints the picture of men who play with the glorious purposes of God, who flaunt them by neglect and open disdain, whose sin is the deep dye of their own selfish pride. And yet its picture is brightest when it looks darkest, for the gift of God's own Son for the life of the world, much as it seems to put God at the disposal of men and bring about the defeat of his good will, is the very means of triumphing over the hard hearts of men and so fulfilling his purpose in glory.

Now it is only when people go to the Bible, understanding that it has this story of real and yet ideal things to tell, that they get from it any true meaning. It is because so many lack the grasp of what the Bible starts out to do that they think of it as a hard or cold or meaningless volume. To those who do not feel the need of its passion for redemption, the Bible remains closed.

The other main reason that so many Protestant families do not relish the Bible is that they just do not understand how to go about reading or using it. Many of them have sincerely tried, but have given up in despair. They have opened the Bible together in their homes and have tried to read it, only to find so much of it hard to understand, so much apparently foreign to the needs and problems of their lives, that they have laid it aside again. Closed Bibles that adorn living-room tables tell mute stories, not alone of disinterest, but of disappointment. To many, even of the fairly well educated, the Bible just does not make sense, and it is not primarily their fault that this is so.

For one thing, there is no explanation in the book of how it came to be. Any other book on the churchman's table will contain the author's preface, explanatory of why it was written, and of the order of its contents. But here is a volume containing sixty-six books with no word as to how they came together or why. The books do not appear in anything like the order in which they were written. That they were gathered together by the church in this form at some date in the distant past the reader may be dimly aware, but how this came about is a matter of guess on his part. The common answer has been, "The Holy Spirit guided the church in this work, both in the selection and order of the books, and the Holy Spirit will interpret them to you." This is true, but it is no excuse for keeping present-day Christians in ignorance of the reasons which the church of an earlier day had for believing they were guided by the Spirit, nor does it excuse idleness on the part of the church in interpreting the Bible today. The complacent doctrine of the guidance of the

Spirit may become Protestantism's tool for keeping the people in ignorance as much as Catholicism's dictum of the church's word that must be taken without reason.

For another thing, there is no connection evident between many of the books. Perhaps the average reader will readily see why Exodus follows Genesis, or Samuel precedes Kings, but he certainly cannot be expected to guess why Job follows Esther or Isaiah the Song of Solomon. What is the meaning of the arrangement of the books, in what order should he read them, and what connecting message can he expect to find between them all?

But perhaps worse than these things, the average Christian will find the Bible an uninviting book to take up in his hands. In most versions its pages have two columns, while every other book he owns has but a one-column page. It is divided into very short chapters, inducing him to stop reading before he has got fairly started. These divisions often interrupt the real connection of thought. Still worse, the chapters are broken up into verses, whose recurrent numbers suggest single isolated thoughts that would make the Bible a mere collection of good sayings instead of a connected narrative or theme, as it generally is. If he follows only the King James Version, the reader will note that each verse stands in a paragraph to itself, magnifying the apparent lack of connected thought.

Such conditions are in part the product of an age that did not believe help in understanding the Bible was needed or desirable. Giving the Bible to the people "without note or comment" became a mere fetish. Many people went so far as to feel that the more difficult and mysterious the Word of God seemed, the more it honored his awful and revered Name. But such a position is entirely inconsistent with the idea of giving the Bible to the people at all. If people are to have the Bible they should have it, not alone in their own language, but in the most intelligible and inviting form possible. That which is mysterious is not therefore more awe-inspiring The hidden and the spiritual are not necessarily one. The Bible is meant to be an open book, completely revealing the Word of God as it grew in the lives of men until it came to full light in Jesus Christ. Reading it should be made easy and even inevitable.

The purpose of the present volume is to suggest some ways of reading the Bible that will help to make it glow with meaning. An examination needs to be made of current practices, of various possible uses of the best methods, and of tools for the reader that will be as sharp as the tools of the worker. Comprehending the Bible may not be immediately easy to those unskilled in its methods of thought, but it is surprising how much a little attention to simple principles and procedures will help. "Seek and read from the book of the Lord" (Isa. 34: 16). We may well seek long until we can answer in the affirmative Philip's question to the Ethiopian, "Do you understand what you are reading?" (Acts 8: 30).

Chapter 2

THE KEY TO GOOD READING

If "reading maketh a full man," as Bacon insisted, then surely those who are disciples of him who came to bring fullness of life ought to be great readers. And if the Bible is truly what we have always claimed it is, the lamp of God to our feet, then the Christian church ought to be filled with those who joyfully search it out.

But, in addition to the fact that the Bible seems unattractive and unintelligible to many, we have to face the sobering reality that so many *do not know how to read.* Such a statement is not, of course, intended to imply that any appreciable number of the church's adherents do not "know letters"; but an acquaintance with words is not the sole requirement for reading. Many people who feel they read a great deal actually get but little out of it, and most of us need to learn some elementary principles if we would get good results.

PRINCIPLES OF GOOD READING

Certain of these principles are true, not only in relation to the Bible, but of the reading of an essay, a poem, a novel, or even a newspaper. Reading consists in getting the thought appreciatively, so that one sees what the author is driving at and what is his point of view. Such reading is not done by a slavish following of words, nor by a painful analysis of the thought, unless in the case of some abstract treatise that is very hard to understand. Rather it means the getting of the spirit and the message as a whole. This can be missed by too slow or careful a reading, just as readily as by haste or carelessness.

9

It is necessary, on the one hand, to think of what one is doing, to put other things out of one's mind, noting the beauty of style and the development of thought as one proceeds. On the other hand one needs to read fast enough and in sufficient quantities to get really interested, and to keep details of the reading itself or distractions from the outside from spoiling the results. Other things being equal, that which is read alertly, quickly, and with full attention, means more and is better retained than that which is pored over by a plodding, "faithful" reader, or that which is done in snatches by one who skips through. These familiar facts need re-emphasis every time one takes up a book. They are of great importance in reading the Book of books.

But the use of the Bible has also developed a special set of sins and follies that need correction. Many well-meaning people seldom pick up their Bibles except when they are tired and sleepy and ready for bed, and then wonder why the words do not leap out at them in the way they did from the pages of the story read two hours earlier or from the television screen they followed so closely. For the Bible has many stories and pictures and in spite of the archaic language and other drawbacks in the style of our King James Version, it catches the imagination if given half a chance. But how many intelligent Christians drop down on the arm of a chair to finger nervously over a page of the Bible for a few minutes, half in satisfaction of a conscientious scruple that they ought to be reading it, and half in pathetic longing for something, they know not exactly what! They have read their evening paper in the comfort of their best lounge chair, and with all the deliberateness that any writer could desire. It is out of halfhearted habits that the excuses of "not enough time" or "can't understand it" frequently arise. The approach and posture in Bible reading can make all the difference between drudgery and pleasure.

But after all, how do you read? Assuming that you give an honest chance to the message of the Bible, how do you go about getting acquainted with it? There are many methods of reading that are followed by Christians. Each has its good points, but most of the popular ones have also their serious drawbacks.

COMMON METHODS OF BIBLE READING

There is the custom of reading by verses picked at random. You leaf here and there through the Bible, and read whatever you happen to open to, or whatever strikes your fancy. And you sometimes get a good thought that way. You are in a certain mood, and the message of a Bible passage strikes you directly. You catch a thought as it soars on the wing, and it is evermore memorable in connection with the occasion on which you read it. You may even mark a date in your Bible at the point to which you turned, and you may feel that you were divinely guided to open the book at that point.

That the blessings of God may at times descend upon casual and fleeting use of scripture is as true as the certainty that spontaneous, importunate prayer in the midst of dire extremity may be real. But one who limits himself to that kind of prayer will learn little of the blessedness of abiding fellowship with God, which is the highest essence of prayer. And one who trusts entirely to *random* reading will get little of the real message of the Bible, or of its full-orbed worth for his life. He is trusting the greatest book in the world to chance, and though, on occasion when his need is real, God may speak to him through that chance, generally he gets nothing at all.

Worse than that, such a reader often misleads himself, for he will take a verse from the Psalms and then turn over to Paul, putting two things together that have no immediate connection. Some striking similarity may lead him to think he sees a relationship, but he tends to combine two quite different subjects. Before long he may be off on a tangent. Many of the sects and isms that beset American Christianity have come about in just this way. The principle that "scripture is to be interpreted by scripture" is no more a blanket rule to apply to all thinking about the Bible than it would be to interpret a sentence in the editorial column of the morning newspaper by an account on the sports page. One might find an editorial about some sport, but unless one does the two have no connection. The whole practice of casually reading the Bible in this hit-and-miss way grows out of understanding the book to be a collection of texts —a misunderstanding implanted in many Christians unconsciously by much of our random type of preaching and our piecemeal theology that seeks to establish some tenet by a verse of scripture. It is this habit that has led some people to say contemptuously, "You can prove anything by the Bible."

A second popular way of reading the Bible is by *chapter divisions*. This may be done in order or again, as with the verses, at random. Now sometimes a chapter of the Bible is a unit in itself and a real message may come from this way of reading, as for example, Isaiah 55 with its gracious invitation. But more often a chapter belongs in a larger setting—a story or a discussion or a teaching. To stop at the end of the second chapter of the Gospel of Mark, just because it is the end of a chapter, is to stop in the midst of Jesus' interpretation of the Sabbath to the Pharisees of the Galilean synagogues. To begin at the beginning of even so famous a chapter as the thirteenth of I Corinthians is to miss the point out of which it grows in the last few verses of the twelfth. The twentieth chapter of Exodus with its presentation of the Ten Commandments has suffered greatly by being severed from the nineteenth, which describes the setting of awe in the midst of which the commandments were given. Chapter divisions, like verse divisions, are an expedient of the church, devised in the Middle Ages for convenience of reference, but never intended as stopping points in reading. They sometimes represent happy divisions in the thought and they sometimes do not. At least one chapter (Acts 22) even begins in the middle of a sentence.

Again, there are many devout souls who read the Bible *straight through* from beginning to end in portions of varying length. This method, too, has its values. The reader is at least sure that he is not habitually slighting any part, and that he has read it all, though this may take so long that he has forgotten much of the first part by the time he nears the end. It is at best an artificial plan. Since the books

of the Bible are not chronologically arranged, there is often no special thought connection to be found in going from one of them to
the next. There would often be much greater value in turning to a
book in another part of the Bible that is more closely related. Judges
and Ruth, occurring together, do indeed fit beautifully, as the story
of Ruth is placed in the times of the judges. For the same reason,
the prophecies of Amos and Hosea should be read with the middle
portion of II Kings, since the history of their times is there described.
There are, as we shall see, definite reasons for the occurrence of the
books as we have them. We are not suggesting that the order is
hodgepodge. Indeed, if one knows why he is doing it, he may read
the books of the Bible with profit in exactly the order in which they
occur. But there is little particular value in going through them
thus without understanding why they were placed in this order in
the canon.

Moreover, in reading the Bible straight through, the average person fails to get the emphases that he needs. He will read the genealogical tables in Matthew and Luke with the thoroughness that he
gives to the same Gospels' presentation of the Sermon on the
Mount. He is in danger of treating the entire Bible as a fetish, to be
devoutly read through, whether or no; and this is a way, not of hon-
oring the Bible, but of dishonoring it. Above all, he is likely to fall
a prey to the various schemes for reading the Bible through in a
year, or in three years, or in some other exact period of time—
schemes that result in slavery to the letter of a task rather than in
the joy of a real accomplishment.

Sometimes, studious people try to follow a guide for reading the
Bible by topics, as a corrective to the lack of emphasis in reading it
straight through. But here again, whatever values may be gained
are decidedly limited by the artificiality of the pursuit. For men
do not live by topics. You cannot trace purity through the Bible,
and then love, and then truthfulness, and then something else, and
get a good life by adding them all together. Not only are you bound
to miss much because you never can get enough topics, but you fail
to see related thought that is couched in different language. You

are like the man who traced the thought of sacrifice through the Bible in this way and omitted the fifth chapter of Revelation with its wonderful picture of the Lamb, standing as though it had been slain. That glorious chapter happens not to contain the word "sacrifice," though it is one of the finest illustrations in scripture of that theme.

Even reading by *books* in carefully selected order will not always produce the sense of a unified thought. A book of the Bible by no means always confines itself to a single theme. Paul's letter to the Galatians does, and can well be read at a single sitting and as one thought. But Paul's second letter to the Corinthians, though not long, contains three distinct themes, quite separated in thought and purpose.

READING BY UNITS OF THOUGHT

The best of all ways to read the Bible with satisfaction is by *units of thought*. A Bible that is well paragraphed, and one in which the chapters and verses do not stand out too prominently, will help greatly in this. For the paragraph of writing represents more nearly than anything else the way people think. This is one good reason for developing the habit of reading from the Revised Standard Version. It is printed by paragraphs and thus helps the reader see the connection of the thought. While some editions of the King James Version make use of paragraph signs, each verse is printed as a separate paragraph.

But the reader should be able to see more than the beginning and ending of separate small paragraphs of thought. He must catch something of the purpose and method of the writers. If, for example, you are familiar with the sermonizing intent of Matthew, you know why all that Jesus said on Righteousness is gathered together in one great discourse which we call "The Sermon on the Mount," though you will find most of the same material scattered over eleven chapters of the Gospel of Luke in the form of short sayings connected with special occasions. If you know the surprising depths of Paul's patriotism, you understand why chapters 9–11 of his letter to the Romans belong together. *A unit of thought is any passage, however long or short, that naturally belongs together, and should be read and understood together because it deals with just one theme.* In much of the book of Proverbs, though not in all, each separate verse is a unit of thought by itself, and therefore reading by verses is quite in order. You can begin anywhere and stop anywhere; it does not matter much. But in the book of Judges, the story of Samson, chapters 13–16, is one connected unit of thought, and it is absurd to stop short of these four chapters in reading. To one who has never tried it, the effect of completing a story from the Bible at a sitting comes with a thrill of surprise, and often produces an enthusiasm for Bible reading that transforms life habits.

But the average layman needs help, and a good deal of it, if he is going to read his Bible in such a way. Sometimes the units of thought stand out very clearly. Again, they are obscured. Almost anyone can tell that the 114th Psalm is a poem in itself descriptive of the exodus of Israel from Egypt. It takes only a little closer observation to see that the forty-third Psalm should always be read as an additional stanza to the forty-second. But the average reader will hardly discern that the immortal rhapsody of Isaiah, chapters 40–66, a unit in itself in some ways, contains, none the less, three distinct divisions of thought. Once shown this, the reader readily learns to appreciate these separate parts of this great masterpiece.

Chapter 3

READING A BOOK AS A BOOK

The Bible is a small volume. It will amaze the rather casual reader to discover in how brief a time most of its books can be covered. And brevity is not alone the soul of wit, but also much of the charm of sacred writing. The very fact that the Gospels obviously omit so much of the detailed activity of Jesus or that the historical books of the Old Testament leave so much to the imagination invites one to read on. A modern dramatist would string out to far greater length such a scene as that of Moses at the burning bush or Jesus walking on the water, but the Bible is content to picture the acts of God in history in terms of brief but significant episodes.

Wherever it is possible, it is desirable to read at a sitting those books of the Bible which are in themselves units of thought. In this way the flow of a single stream of ideas is not interrupted and often sweeps in upon the heart.

The time required to read many of the books of the Bible at a sitting is really very slight. Making ample allowance for leisureliness and even for oral reading, more than half of the sixty-six books can be read in an average of about twenty minutes each, no one of them requiring more than an hour. These include:

From the Old Testament:

The five "rolls": Ruth, Esther, Ecclesiastes, Song of Solomon, Lamentations.

The twelve "Minor Prophets": Hosea, Joel, Amos, Obadiah, Jonah, Micah, Nahum, Habakkuk, Zephaniah, Haggai, Zechariah, Malachi.

From the New Testament:

> Ten of Paul's Letters: Galatians, Ephesians, Philippians, Colossians, I Thessalonians, II Thessalonians, I Timothy, II Timothy, Titus, Philemon.
>
> The seven "General" or "Catholic" Letters: James, I Peter, II Peter, I John, II John, III John, Jude.

The more rapid reader will find that to the list of these that can be read in an hour or less he will quickly add such letters as Hebrews, II Corinthians, and even I Corinthians, and such an Old Testament book as Daniel. Speed is not, of course, the only object in reading the Bible, nor is it the main one. Reading a book through in a certain length of time may be done more as a stunt than anything else; churches have read the entire New Testament through in an evening, often in the spirit of seeing if they can do it. Nevertheless, it is a rewarding experience to take any of the above list as a single unit in the same way that one would a thirty-minute article or an hour's magazine story.

Many readers of the Bible have had rich experiences in completing at a single sitting books that are longer than an hour's reading time. Especially do the Gospels appeal in a new way when read as single units of thought.

When we examine the question of what different kinds of books are best treated as units of thought, the first thing that strikes us is that they all have to do in some way with a story. It is the story interest that makes most teaching live, and the writers of the books of the Bible have demonstrated this truth abundantly.

THE HERO STORY BOOK

There is, for example, the hero story. Many of the longer books of the Bible, such as Genesis or Judges, are made up of collections of such hero stories, and their units of thought are clearly seen from a list of the names of those whose exploits they record. But certain books have to do altogether with one hero, or, more often (oddly enough, perhaps), with one heroine. We shall examine two Old Testament cases.

There is the book of Ruth. This delightful little pastoral in prose,
this idyl of the home, is spoiled by dividing it into four chapters.
The picture is too vivid to be a good continued story; it needs to be
seen all at once. The utter dejection of the withered old Naomi; the
self-abnegating loyalty of the young and attractive Ruth; the des-
perate attempt to make a living and to find a place in Naomi's old
home; the courtly surprise and chaste approaches of the man of the
Lord's destiny—Boaz, kindly, and of careful dealing; the sudden and
glorious conclusion—all these are marks of progress, but not of division, in this lovely story. Behind the deep emotion that is evident,
one sees passing by many of the everyday scenes of the days of the
judges: famine driving people from a settled life; acquiescence in
union with foreign peoples; customs of travel and of home life; customs of the fields; and especially the danger to young women in
those times when "there was no law in the land," and when the repeated statement of the book of Judges that "every man did that
which was right in his own eyes" (17: 6; 21: 25) became only a refined way of saying that every man did what he desired. The noble
romantic element in the story is all the more picturesque against
the quaint background of the threshing floor and the court scene
at the town gate. It should be noted that this brief book manages
to sketch with exquisite skill scenes from home life, from industry,
from legal dealings, from social fellowship, from sale of property.
Very evident is the religious background of it all even where no form
of worship is introduced, as seen in such a note as the formal greet-
ing of friends who meet (2: 4), the protective benediction of Boaz
to Ruth (2: 12), and the prayer for the Lord's blessing on the union
of the two lovers (4: 11, 12, 14). This little book is a unit of thought.

There is the book of Esther. This can indeed be read as a continued story as Ruth cannot. With all the queenliness of Esther
there is something very feminine about her. She uses her woman's
arts to bring the king to her way and accomplish her dangerous
mission. Among these arts are not only her beauty and the effective-
ness of her personality, but her skill in creating expectancy. Esther
knows how to build up her plans and to cause just those delays that

will give time for the gathering momentum of her forces. Truly her astute cousin understood her as well as the purpose of God when he said, "And who knows whether you have not come to the kingdom for such a time as this?" (4: 14). Esther's policy of delay is best seen when she bids Haman and the king to a banquet and whets their curiosity by bidding them to another before she will speak her mind (ch. 5). Taking his cue from her policy the author seems to organize his story of her around delayed or interrupted incidents, especially in the earlier parts, and if one desires, the story may be broken at these points for reading. Thus each of the first three chapters can be read separately, the brilliant account of the great feast when Vashti was deposed as queen, the tale of the rise of Esther, and the fall of the tricky Haman. Chapters 4 and 5 must go together as the plot of Esther aided by Mordecai. Chapter 6 is the really artistic break in the story, the one place where a modern author would delightedly write, "To be continued." Here, between the first and second banquets that Esther gives is the interlude of the king's sleepless night. From there on the story runs more evenly to its conclusion, and the remainder should be read without pause. Of course, the entire book may easily be read as a unit, for the imagination can readily allow for the effect of Esther's policy of interruption.

STORY BOOKS OF PROPHETS

But not only the books that present heroes or heroines are noteworthy as story units. There are certain writings which we number among the prophets that are quite obviously single stories.

The book of Jonah readily suggests itself. Perhaps this is more often thought of as a unit than most of the others, although the tendency to stop with its curiosities blinds the eyes of many to the fact that here is one of the great missionary tracts of all time. It is very definitely a teaching book. Its message is summed up in its closing question, "Should not I pity Nineveh?" The great heart of God revealed here should not be stilled by debates on the historicity of the character of Jonah or the date of the book, or the question of whether the story of the great fish and the preaching in Nineveh are to be taken literally or only symbolically. The book is didactic, as the closing question shows. In effect that question asks, "Cannot other peoples share in the love of God?"

Here is the living epic of a man called to be a preacher—a missionary who, like so many others of later day, did not want to respond. And his unwillingness had a mixture of personal desire and patriotic feeling and (hard to realize!) religion as he understood it. "Arise, go to Nineveh, . . . and proclaim to it the message that I tell you," came the voice of the Lord. "Yet forty days, and Nineveh shall be overthrown." But that was just what Jonah wanted to happen. Had not Nineveh been most cruel of Israel's enemies? What greater glory to the righteousness of Israel's God than the overthrow of Nineveh? Now the easy conclusion would be that Jonah did not know well enough the mercy of the Lord. But the point of the story is that he knew it too well. He knew it far better than he wanted to. It was from the idea of the Lord's universal mercy that Jonah ran away. And he took ship in exactly the opposite direction from Nineveh, and "he paid the fare" in more senses than one. The drama of the deep sea and the far distant dry land is the awakening of Jonah, not to a belief in God's mercy—he does not desire that any more than he did at first—but to the inevitableness of that mercy. He goes to Nineveh and preaches with the most fatalistic feeling any preacher ever had, and when things come out as he knew they would, he sulks and is angry at his fate. Behold a preacher who grieves because men have listened to his preaching and have turned to God! It is the absurdity of this situation that Jonah must be shown. The story of the gourd that grew up in Jonah's retreat outside the city walls which was beloved by him because it meant much to him becomes the parable by which the Lord may at last bring home to the unwilling prophet how much the people of Nineveh and even its cattle mean to him.

Now all the movement of the story of Jonah is missed if one stops reading at the end of any of the book's four short chapters. The book itself is but a leaf, and needs to be read at one sitting, and fairly rapidly, to make its message glow. Similarly, with such prophetic stories as those of Habakkuk, Joel, and Zephaniah, division tends to spoil the message.

INTERPRETATIONS OF LIFE STORIES

So far, we have been considering story books of the Bible that can best be read each as one narrative. But there are other books which are essentially story interpretations, and which also mean more if read as a unit with the story element prominent.

Take, for example, Paul's Letter to the Galatians. What could be further from a story, someone asks? Is not this the deep theological treatise out of which Protestantism grew? Yet, back of this seemingly theoretical writing is the burning passion of a life, and the letter is in reality the interpretation of that story. Saul, the zealous persecutor of the church, has become Paul the even more zealous apostle of the faith. But that faith is questioned, as is his apostleship, and that in the church itself. It would seem that one who before his conversion had spurned the apostles and belied the faith would be kind and patient with those who were doing the same things now, but not thus does the course of human character run. Those who have been the hardest to win often become the most intolerant of others who still cannot see the light. It is the greatness of their own change that makes them so. The gospel has done so much for them that they can brook no failure to see it in its richness. So the passion and intolerance of Paul break forth at their keenest in this letter directed to the Galatian region where the gospel of faith and the reality of Paul's own apostleship are being the most questioned. To get the full sweep of that passion, and appreciate the reasonableness of that intolerance, the letter needs to be read at a sitting. The writer will never forget his own experience, when, as a college youth, he sat down one day and read in fifteen minutes this fiery note of Christianity's beginnings. The thrill that came over him drew him into the ardor of the apostle so potently that the glow has never died.

As with the life of Paul, so with that of Jesus. It is related as a story interpretation, though not entirely so in the Gospel of Matthew, nor yet in the Gospel of John. But then, one would not look for the interpretation of Paul's life as a story in his letter to the Romans or to the Ephesians. Galatians fulfills its unique purpose here. And so with the life of Jesus. The Gospels of Mark and Luke present story interpretations of that life, and of these the Gospel of Mark is the better illustration.

I was once asked to substitute in a Sunday school class of ten or a dozen Junior boys. The boys had a view of Jesus common among those of Junior age, that he was a sort of sissy loved by women and little children. I asked them if they would be fair enough to do just one thing: read the first two chapters of the Gospel of Mark and see what they thought of Jesus. I even dared them not to come back to Sunday school unless they had read those chapters. The boys took the dare and read and came. Most of them had some warmth of feeling in their response the next Sunday. I asked them what impression of Jesus they got. One of them summed up his feelings by answering, "He sure got over the ground fast." An expert theologian could hardly have done better. The whole point of view of Mark's gospel is the painting of a picture of rapid movement. It is a sound film of the great hero Jesus. There is little chronology, but rather a portrayal of what sort of person he was by the leaping story of his work. No wonder a city newspaper editor said he required all his cub reporters to read the Gospel of Mark in order to learn how to tell a story that would get the headlines and make the first page!

Perhaps the grandest section of the Gospel is that from 4: 35 through 5: 43. Here we have the Master of life presented to us in four moving stories which ought all to be in one chapter. He is first the master of the storm in nature, then of the storm in the demoniac mind, then of the storm of shrinking in the sick woman's timid soul, then of the storm of death in the household of the ruler. But, this is only an unusually good example of the sort of thing that is to be found throughout Mark's brief account: not merely a narrative, but an interpretation by realistic story, of the life and character of Jesus. Anyone who reads the Gospel of Mark thus, at one sitting, has in store for him a new entrance into the heart of the Master, a real vision of Jesus as though he were here in the flesh.

Chapter 4

READING A BOOK
ACCORDING TO ITS STORY DIVISIONS

In the last chapter we considered what it means to read as a unit a book of the Bible that contains just one story or is an interpretation of just one story. But there are many books of the Bible that deal with more than one story. Many of these would be too long to finish at a single sitting unless one devoted considerable time to the reading. But they can be appreciated rather easily by learning to divide them at the point of their passing from one story to another.

STORY UNITS OF CHARACTERS

Among these books, the easiest to handle are those that are built around the lives of heroes. Just as books like Ruth and Esther offer the story unit of the single hero, so books like Genesis and Judges offer a number of story units grouped around the characters of famous men.

Take Genesis for example. If one can trace the activity of God in the life story of Adam, Noah, Abraham, Isaac, Jacob, and Joseph, he knows the book of Genesis. He does not even need to make an exception of the story of creation, for this is artistically told as part of the story of Adam. The universe was made for man. Indeed, one of the most disastrous mistakes that can be made in reading the book of Genesis is to pin the mind on the narrative of events rather than on the stories of God's use of the lives of men. The events are narrated to trace the development of the characters of the men who are the heirs of God's covenant. The creation finds its purpose in the God image in Adam. The flood finds its higher purpose in the contrasting picture of the righteousness of Noah. The growth of the faithful Abram from his leaving Ur to his worship at Bethel, from his sojourning in Egypt to his offering up of the son of promise, is central in importance to a large section of Genesis. The development of Jacob from his early days with Isaac and Rebekah and Esau to his good bargain at Bethel, from his crafty management of Laban's affairs to his real change in the wrestling at Peniel, is the story of the unfolding of a life under the hand of God. The early interest in the boyhood of Joseph with his dreams and his fancies issues in the closing chapters of Genesis which are the epic of a man who never doubted God's good intent for his life.

It is a great mistake to let one's interest in the book of Genesis center in a debate about the nature of the creation, or the relation of the flood to flood stories in Babylonian literature, or the question as to whether the movements of Abraham represent those of a tribe, or the historical relation of the stories of Joseph to the dynasties of the Egyptian Pharaohs. As will be noted in a later chapter dealing with outlines of Biblical books, the watershed of Genesis is the account of the tower of Babel in chapter 11. This story may not seem to center in persons, and it is indeed the point of transfer from the book's concern with the world in general to the family of Israel. Yet, even at Babel, the real interest is in the character of the men that caused the unity of human life to fail. As a matter of fact the whole book of Genesis is quite comparable in literary style and method of procedure with such works as the *Iliad* and the *Aeneid*, and it may be said to be a series of epics of great lives. What the wanderings of Ulysses under the guidance of his very human deities were to the authors of the classics, the wanderings of Abraham under the providential hand of the God of all the earth were to the writer of Genesis, and he narrated them with the same passionate devotion to his hero. The reader of the first book of the Bible will learn to know God's use of human character if he divides his reading of the book into just the five or six divisions that mark off its great men.

Why say five or six? Because there is some question whether the
stories of Isaac should be considered a separate cycle. It is told that
Abraham Mendelssohn used to say smilingly, "I am nobody; I am
only the son of Moses Mendelssohn, the philosopher, and the father
of Felix Mendelssohn, the musician." In a similar way, Isaac appears
in the book of Genesis as the son of Abraham and the father of
Jacob. It will be noted that practically all the stories of Isaac are
told with reference to one of the other two. He "dug again the wells
of water which had been dug in the days of Abraham his father,"
sums up Isaac's early life as a peaceful shepherd. His wooing is done
for him by his father's servant. His household is dominated by his
wife Rebekah. His last days are noteworthy only as they determine
the lot of his son Jacob. An Abraham cycle there certainly is; a
Jacob cycle is equally distinct; but Isaac fades into the mist between
the two.

The most fascinating of all the cycles of the book of Genesis is
that of Joseph. The story runs in spectacular development from
chapter 37 to the end of the book, though it contains by contrast in
chapter 38 the story of the lechery of Jacob's sons. This complete
epic of Joseph can easily be read in an hour or less, thus taking its
place with the list of books drawn up at the beginning of chapter 3.
Yet how few Christians have ever read the story as one! The division
into thirteen different chapters makes it look like a stupendous task,
and scores of good people who think nothing of an hour's magazine story have never really read the life of Joseph. Yet there are
few stories in literature more rewarding. The effect of the prophetic
dreams, of the prolonged deceit of Joseph's brothers, of the travail
of Jacob's soul, of the convergence of circumstances in Egypt and
Canaan, of the play of the will of God upon the doings of men, of
the piteousness of the famine-stricken family, of Joseph's deep
understanding of the meaning and requirements of forgiveness—all
these and many more, well known though they are, when read as
elements in one connected story quicken the spirit with a new
delight. For the life of Joseph as narrated in the Bible is one of the
best told stories in all the world, and the religious interpretation of

history which it unfolds is both charming and convincing. Modern novelists and dramatists now vie with each other in letting their imaginations play upon it.

In a similar way the book of Judges should be read, not as separate chapters, nor as a series of disconnected events, but as groups of stories of heroes, each a unit in its own right. Thus it will become evident that the fourth and fifth chapters belong together, for in them are the prose narrative and the poetical description of the deliverance wrought for Israel by Deborah. Again, the seventh, eighth, and ninth chapters ought to be read as one, for they contain the tales of Gideon and his family. Chapters 13 through 16 are a unit in themselves on the exploits of Samson, and so on.

STORY UNITS OF OCCASIONS

But not all of the longer books can be divided for reading according to the various characters who are prominent. Sometimes there is only one outstanding character in all the book, and the units of thought are important occasions in his life or in the life of the people he leads. The book of Deuteronomy is a case in point. It is, as its name implies, the "second law," not in the sense that it is a new law, but that it is a fresh recital, a new interpretation, of the law in terms of great occasions in the life of Israel. The book definitely states these occasions and represents them as being made great by Moses' re-interpretations of the law. Deuteronomy is the written record of what purports to be spoken rhetoric, one of the finest examples of the rhetorical style in all literature. The book should be read, then, according to these occasions of its spoken messages. The divisions are clearly marked in the book itself.* Such a procedure will, of course, divide the reading into quite unequal sections. One of these will be long, but it is of such nature that to stop here and there in it and then take it up again will not mean to lose the thread of contact. The book, read in this way, will appeal

* For this and all other detailed illustrations of the divisions of books of the Bible, see the outlines in chapters 7 and 8.

especially for its fine insight into the needs of human nature, its stress on the humanitarian character of Israel's law, and its noble consciousness of God's justice and mercy.

STORY UNITS OF PROPHETIC VISIONS

There is another type of book, often longer, in which neither different characters nor distinct occasions serve as the natural divisions. The books of the Old Testament prophets are richly rewarding when they are read in an intelligent fashion. It is a shame to leave them to the sense of mystery which so often surrounds them, or to the interest of those alone who overemphasize their predictions or give them some bizarre interpretation. It is, of course, not always possible for the average reader of the Bible to understand the historical background of the prophet's message. Needed help can be found in dictionaries and commentaries. But the place to begin is not with outside helps, but always with the Bible itself. In the case of the prophets, learning to start and stop with a new prophetic vision is the beginning of wisdom. The prophets preached, or taught, only when they had a particular "burden" or "vision," and the markings of new messages are usually to be noted in some such words as these.

Among the "Minor," that is, the shorter, books of the prophets, Amos makes a good example. As has already been pointed out, the entire book can be read in less than an hour. Yet it also contains shorter units. The book is a collection of brief oracles of a desert preacher. Even the inexperienced reader will soon note that the first two chapters are alike with their oft-repeated phrase, "For three transgressions [of such and such a people], and for four, I will not revoke the punishment." This is the refrain of most of the eight or ten short stanzas of the poem of judgment which composes the first two chapters.

The Revised Standard Version helps the reader by giving a double paragraph break at the beginning of the third chapter of the book of Amos, and again at the seventh chapter. But even without this help, most readers would soon see that the material from chapter 3 through chapter 6 is in quite similar tone and style, and quite different from the first two chapters. It will do anyone good to read chapters 3–6 without stopping, but, if one desires still more breaks, he will soon learn to make them, regardless of chapter divisions, at the points where typical prophetic introductions occur: "Hear this word," or simply, "Hear," or "Thus says the Lord."

The last three chapters of the prophecy of Amos, 7–9, have still a different ring. Recurring throughout them is the pointer, "Thus the Lord God showed me." Object after object is brought in by Amos and used symbolically to interpret various visions which the Lord has showed him. The prophets did a good deal of preaching of this kind.

The Bible reader will soon get interested in the works of the prophets if he seeks for such marks of prophetic messages. The quest has all the interest of a hunt, with the sermons of the prophet as reward. In the case of Amos, the hunt will take one through vivid paragraphs of vision of the nation's sins and of God's judgment, with the rural figures of the prophet from the hills echoing down the choked streets of the cities where he thundered forth his oracles.

Among the "Major," that is, the longer, books of the prophets, Isaiah may serve as an illustration of the units of prophetic vision. The first five chapters are very much in the style of Amos, displaying the sins of the people of Judah. Here the common phrases recur: "The vision of Isaiah"; "The word which Isaiah the son of Amoz saw"; "Woe to those. . . ." These are marks of new oracles, and though they divide these chapters into very short passages, they are convenient guides in reading.

With the beginning of chapter 6, where the famous call of Isaiah occurs, the reader will note a somewhat new style. Now the notes of time become suggestive of natural breaks: "In the year that king Uzziah died"; "In the days of Ahaz"; "In that day." This kind of prophecy, running through chapter 12, has in it several different

sorts of visions and a remarkable dirge-poem (9: 8–10: 4) where the
reader will readily pick out the oft-repeated refrain,

> For all this his anger is not turned away,
> and his hand is stretched out still.

It will be still easier to follow Isaiah in chapters 13–23, where the
recurring mark of division is the word "oracle." These chapters are
mostly visions of doom on foreign nations, and it is convenient to
have these samples of Isaiah's preaching collected in this fashion.

With the twenty-eighth chapter the prophet returns to his earlier
style, and from 28–35 there is a series of oracles where the lights of
God's mercy and the shadows of the national sin play across each
other. Here the common words that mark natural divisions of
thought are "Behold," "In that day," "Woe to ———," and the
like. There follows a short historical narrative, chapters 36–39, quite
similar to one in the book of Kings, where any reader can tell that
he would be making a grave mistake to interrupt himself short of
completing this story of Hezekiah's wrestling with the practical
problems of faith as they were preached to him by Isaiah.

Most readers of the Bible are aware that chapters 40–66 of the
book of Isaiah form a section to themselves, with quite different
mood and message from the first thirty-nine chapters. Here, the
picture of the exile is poetically drawn and the rich promises of
restoration are developed. Here also there appear the alternating
themes of the greatness of God and the call of his "Servant." It
will not be so easy to decide where best to make breaks in the reading, nor is it so important, since the majestic flow of the thought
and imagery of these chapters is so evenly sustained. Most people
who have had experience in Bible reading like to divide these
chapters into three groups. Some of them find the units of the
prophet's visions marked off by the repeated saying at the end of
chapters 48 and 57, "There is no peace . . . for the wicked." Others
find a more natural division to be: "The glorious might of God,"
40–47; "The graciousness of God's invitation," 48–55; "The new call
to righteousness," 56–66. Within such limits as these one may stop

almost anywhere he finds it necessary, though the reading of long parts without pause will enhance the sense of beauty and majesty which this whole prophecy awakens.

Story Units of Problems

Every now and then one will come across in the Bible books that fall into natural divisions of various problems the author is taking up. In such a way, one may read the attempts of the writer of Ecclesiastes to satisfy his spirit. His varied experiments, and the troubles he finds, are frequently introduced by some such phrase as, "I said to myself," or "Again I saw."

Especially in the letters of the New Testament there may be found a number of illustrations of dealing with church problems as separate units of thought. I Peter and James are good examples, but perhaps the clearest is I Corinthians. One may read this letter of Paul as a collection of bits of sound advice, and may find in it some good doctrine, and beautiful poetry as well, without realizing how the thoughts are fitted together. He is likely to fail to get the real message of the letter from reading it piecemeal. The first four chapters, with their emphasis on the different work of different leaders, and with their seemingly unrelated teaching about the cross of Christ and the wisdom of God, are dealing with just one problem, that of party strife in the Corinthian church. The apostle is trying to solve the division into four parties by showing that the Corinthians are following the worldly wisdom of pride in personalities, while the cross of Christ is God's real wisdom that binds all groups together. Likewise, Paul treats in briefer compass the problems of immorality in the church (ch. 5), of lawsuits among members (ch. 6), and the difficult marriage problems posed by the strenuous times (ch. 7). In fuller development again, he handles the very practical situation arising from the visits of church members to the meat markets of idol temples (chs. 8–10). Such famous sayings as "If food is a cause of my brother's falling, I will never eat meat" (8: 13), and "Let anyone who thinks that he stands take heed lest he fall" (10: 12), are part of the principles by which the apostle is wrestling with this vexing question of right and wrong. These sayings are far more than isolated remarks. And best of all, the great thirteenth chapter of I Corinthians, so often taken out of its setting and made to be only an apostrophe to charity or love, will be clothed with altogether new glory when put back where it belongs in the discussion of the problems of the use of gifts or talents, chapters 12–14. Here Paul, in dealing with a richly endowed church, is trying to help his readers, not only to cherish their gifts in order of importance, but to find in love the spirit in which one may use all abilities and without which any gift is "a noisy gong or a clanging cymbal." These three chapters should always be read together as one of the problem units of this practical, and yet deep-principled, letter.

Story Units of Teaching

It may seem strange to use the word "story" as often as has been done in these pages. But really, all the books of the Bible which we have been considering are stories, looked at from the point of view of their units of thought. Ecclesiastes is a storybook—the fascinating history of a man who sought soul comfort in this way and that. Many of the chapters of Proverbs are the distilling into didactic form of life experiences of men of wisdom.

Especially is this story element illustrated in the Gospels. We have already seen this in the case of Mark with its appeal as a moving narrative of the life of Christ. In quite different sense, this is true of the Gospel of Matthew. This is a "book" in a sense in which Mark is not. It is a carefully constructed series of discourses, or sermons, arranged from the teachings of Jesus and bound together with so much of the narrative of his life as is necessary to give the discourses setting. The things that Jesus did are never of primary importance in the Gospel of Matthew, but rather the things that he taught. And what he taught is seldom to be found as separated little gems of thought rising out of some occasion, or as single parables, after the fashion of Luke, but as clusters of teachings that develop vital themes.

We have long recognized this to be true in Matthew's "Sermon on the Mount." The fifth, sixth, and seventh chapters quite obviously gather together into one discourse a great deal of the teaching of Jesus. Much of this is also to be found in Luke, though there it is scattered throughout many chapters of the Gospel and occurs as separate sayings in conjunction with the occasions on which they were uttered. But in Matthew not only are these sayings grouped around the one occasion of Jesus' teaching on the mountainside; it is also noteworthy that only those are used which fit in with the theme of the righteousness of the members of the kingdom of heaven. "Kingdom Righteousness" might be written as a title for the Sermon on the Mount as we find it in Matthew, and while much good can be got by reading it bit by bit, a new world opens up for the Christian who reads these three chapters at a sitting as he would listen to a sermon from beginning to end.

But the "Sermon on the Mount" is only one of many sermons in the Gospel of Matthew. There is the missionary discourse in chapter 10, one of the most remarkable mission documents in Christian literature. Once again, most of the sayings that occur here are to be found scattered through Luke, but in Matthew they have been gathered together as one sermon on the subject of missions—everything that Jesus ever said on missions, in fact, with the single exception of the "Great Commission" that occurs at the very end of the book. Again, in chapter 11, there is a gathering of materials for a sermon on entering the kingdom—why some come in and others do not, what kind of people find the readiest entrance, and the like.

There is, in Matthew's Gospel, a tendency to group even the parables of Jesus into one connected discourse. This is especially true of the parables of the kingdom, as illustrated in chapter 13. Chapter 18 is also a sermon, made up of many teachings that illustrate humility, the beauty of its grace or the ugliness of life when it is lacking. In chapter 23 there is a sermon of "woes" against the scribes and Pharisees, and in the next two chapters a series of sermons to the disciples on the end of the age and impending judgment. Even the events of passion week, as narrated in Matthew, show the influence of the sermonic element, as they are shot through with groups of teachings of the Master in the temple courts. The best way to read this Gospel is to divide it according to these units of teaching, and thus get the feel of its purpose.

Chapter 5

GETTING AT THE SPIRIT OF A BOOK

Man does not live by thought alone. We have been looking at some of the books of the Bible which may be read as "units of thought." But not all of the sacred literature gives special attention to thought. Some of it is primarily feeling. This is not to disparage any of the sixty-six books, nor is it to say that any one of them is devoid of thought. But it soon becomes evident to the reader of the Bible that, while certain of its books center around some one line of ideas, as has been illustrated in chapter 3, and others around a succession of ideas, as chapter 4 has portrayed, still others can be understood only by entering into their mood. They have come into existence because of a single mood, as in the case of some of the shorter ones, or they are a collection of many moods, as is supremely the case with the Book of Psalms. To lay the stress on thought content is often to miss the purpose of such literature. To learn to feel with the author is to get the real value.

THE UNIT OF A SINGLE MOOD

The prophecy of Nahum is not in the reading canon of a good many Christians. Some who have read it once have dismissed it as impossible for Christian experience. Bitter, vengeful, even vindictive, if this brief message is understood to be final thinking about the way a believer in God may react toward his enemies, then it just does not belong in the same volume with the teaching of Jesus on forgiveness. But the prophecy of Nahum is not teaching at all; it is feeling. It is a magnificent presentation of the spectacle of exultation over the downfall of evil. Its inspiration lies in its faithful picture of aroused righteous indignation.

Consider the position of Nahum. The tyranny of Nineveh had long laid low his people. He had been witness to the grueling fate of men, women, and children, whose blood was the same as his. And Nineveh had looked impregnable. The despair that sits on the shoulder of inevitable fate had been the portion of the Israelites. But now the prophet sees the real weakness of the oppressors. He realizes how soon they must collapse before other rising world powers. The heavy millstone of despair is whisked from his heart by the breath of a whirlwind, and he can but give vent to his pent-up feeling.

"The Lord is a jealous God and avenging," he begins. This may not be the highest way to feel about God, but it is one way that good men frequently do feel. Nahum delights in viewing God's judgment. It is almost with glee that he hears God speak to Nineveh repeatedly, "Behold I am against you" (2: 13; 3: 5). The graphic picture of the coming sack of Nineveh which forms the second chapter of the prophecy echoes the wild cries of bloody warfare as Nineveh gets a taste of her own medicine and seeks frantically to stave off the inevitable. The solemn dirges that close the first and third chapters have about them the irony of deserved destiny. We can understand how the prophet of a righteous God can feel that way, and if we give free rein to our sympathy with him we shall most truly read the book of Nahum.

In far different mood is such a picture of intense feeling as Paul's letter to the Philippians. Here the apostle, who is all too often thought of as a cold logician, lays bare his heart. He is in prison— fettered for the gospel's sake. To put a strong man in chains is sometimes to break his spirit. To tie down an active man is sometimes to make him go mad. But not when his spirit is as joyous in God and as triumphant in faith as is the spirit of Paul; not when a man has the refinement of feeling that can rejoice in what his less capable friends are privileged to do while he is hindered. Such a spirit cannot be imprisoned.

Now, it would be absurd to say that Paul's Letter to the Philippians contains no thought. As a matter fact, it embraces some of Paul's finest theology. The second chapter reflects his deepest thinking about the person of Christ. Yet this comes out incidentally in the expression of a mood. None of it is deliberately planned. It is the creation of spontaneous feeling. To get into the mood of joy and of loving Christian fellowship, and to read this little letter (preferably at one sitting) as the high-water mark in the expression of such joy and fellowship, is to understand it with the heart.

"Have this mind among yourselves, which you have in Christ Jesus" (2: 5), is really the keynote of the letter. It is pre-eminently the New Testament's exhortation to the imitation of Christ. The willingness of Paul to copy his Lord, his humility, his readiness to obey the higher will, his refusal of satisfaction with himself balanced by his contentment with "whatever state"—all these and many more expressions of the mood of following Christ are caught up into the atmosphere of Christian fellowship in which the apostle can most effectively urge his readers, "Brethren, join in imitating me" (3: 17). To get this "mind" is to read Philippians.

The Book of Psalms
and the Range of Human Feeling

Not alone in the shorter books, where one feeling dominates, but in some of the longer ones too, where the range of mood is wide, feeling plays a great rôle in the best reading of the Bible. Of no book is this truer than the longest one. It is a well recognized fact that the book of Psalms nearly runs the gamut of human emotion. Yet this recognition does not always play the part it should in the actual reading of the book. We still ask of this or that Psalm, "Is what it says always true?" when the all-important question is, "Does it portray in a true way to a religious life some ardent feeling of the soul?" This will mean that we shall like some Psalms better than others because we more often enter into the inner chamber of their experience. It will mean that we shall have to learn to like other Psalms whose mood is not so natural to us. It may even mean that some of us will shun a few Psalms whose point of view we do not care to share. But, at all times, we shall strive to follow sympathetically this arterial highway of spiritual emotions. If the Psalmist, exulting in God's providence, declares that he has "not seen the righteous forsaken or his children begging bread" (37: 25), we shall rejoice with him in that spirit, even though we have seen good people go hungry. If the Psalmist proclaims that God has rewarded him according to his righteousness (18: 20, 24), we shall rejoice with him that that was possible and shall seek to avoid the appearance of pride. If the Psalmist imprecates the wrath of God upon his foes, going further than Nahum in begging for wrath that has not yet been decreed, we shall enter the poignancy of his suffering and be humbled by our own impatience rather than by his (137: 7-9). For in spite of the unity of biblical faith, we must never forget that we are New Testament Christians, and that not all the Psalms of the days of the old covenant measure up to the spiritual and moral heights of Christ. But they may still be very valuable; for some of us have not yet caught up to their state of mind, and it will be worth while for all of us to see out of what varieties of religious experience God has brought his people to the full light that is in Jesus Christ. With this in mind, we shall be better fitted to remember that the Psalm Book has been the great source of Christian, as well as of Jewish, devotion.

Now there is much to be gained by reading the Psalms straight through in the Revised Standard Version, where they are all printed as poetry. But, we shall do well to try to group the Psalms according to their differing moods, and to read them in this way many times until their shades of emotion glow for us.

There is no one correct way to classify the Psalms according to the feeling that is dominant. Obviously there are many that express more than one kind of mood. Just as obviously one kind of emotion will often shade over into another, so that it is hard to draw a line between them. Tastes and opinions are bound to differ. Yet it will help tremendously to learn to appreciate a Psalm by what seems to be its dominant mood. Some good helps are suggested in the Bibliography. But for the benefit of those who have nothing but their Bibles before them we are suggesting in detail a classification of the Psalm Book in our chapter on "Reading the Old Testament by Units of Thought." Here our purpose is to illustrate and clarify the meaning of such a classification.

Psalms of Adoration

Perhaps the devout soul seeks first to express exultingly his sense of the greatness of God. He knows his blessings by name, yet they are too numerous to mention. It is not so much the fact that God has favored him in this or that particular way as it is that he has a God who does bless. The Psalter is filled with this type of high devotion.

Many Christians of experience will think first of the hundredth Psalm. Most of us have sung "Old Hundredth" again and again in our churches. It is a very general expression of the mood of adoration. There are few, if any, particular reasons noted, just spontaneous praise:

> Make a joyful noise to the Lord, all the lands!
> . . . .
> Know that the Lord is God!
> . . . .
> we are his people, and the sheep of his pasture.
> . . . .
> For the Lord is good;
> his steadfast love endures for ever,
> and his faithfulness to all generations.

One of the most joyous expressions of adoration is to be found in the forty-seventh Psalm. Here the Psalmist is in glee over the greatness of God, and shout and tumult are needed to express his emotion:

> Clap your hands, all peoples!
>> Shout to God with loud songs of joy!
> For the Lord, the Most High, is terrible,
>> a great king over all the earth.
>
> . . . .
>
> God has gone up with a shout,
>> the Lord with the sound of a trumpet.
> Sing praises to God, sing praises!
>> Sing praises to our King, sing praises!

At other times the spirit of adoration is to be found in quieter mood, as in some shining brooklet moving along with current "too full for sound or foam." Such an expression is that of the sixty-seventh Psalm:

> Let the peoples praise thee, O God;
>> let all the peoples praise thee!
>
> Let the nations be glad and sing for joy,
>> for thou dost judge the peoples with equity
>> and guide the nations upon earth.
>
> . . . .
>
> The earth has yielded its increase;
>> God, our God, has blessed us.
> God has blessed us;
>> let all the ends of the earth fear him!

Psalms of Meditation

In more thoughtful mood are those Psalms which give voice to inner musings of the soul over the meaning of life. Often they end in personal resolve and commitment. Sometimes they pronounce a beatitude upon a certain well-defined type of living.

The very first Psalm comes to mind. Here two ways of life are contrasted, the "way of the righteous" and the "way of the wicked." The one is defined as the way of delight in the law of God and described as the growth of a tree. The other is left undefined, but described as "chaff which the wind drives away." The one is said to be blessed with God's favor, while the other is sure to perish.

Here is a definite teaching element in the Psalms, but growing out of the mood of meditation.

Such a troubled Psalm as the thirty-seventh partakes of the same spirit. Here the Psalmist is meditating, not in serenity, but in fretfulness. The age-old problem of the prosperity of the wicked is bothering him. He seeks to soothe his soul by a series of meditations on the character and outcome of evil men, and from this instructs himself (rather than others) in the way he ought to go:

> Fret not yourself because of the wicked,
>   be not envious of wrongdoers!
> For they will soon fade like the grass,
>   and wither like the green herb.
>
> Trust in the Lord, and do good;
>   so you will dwell in the land, and enjoy security.
> Take delight in the Lord,
>   and he will give you the desires of your heart.
>
> Commit your way to the Lord;
>   trust in him, and he will act.
> . . . .
> Be still before the Lord, and wait patiently for him.
> . . . .
> Better is a little that the righteous has
>   Than the abundance of many wicked.
> . . . .
> The salvation of the righteous is from the Lord.

It will be readily observed how these Psalms of meditation frequently issue in the proverb type of wisdom, as in the last three lines quoted.

Psalms of Trust

The element of trust has been noticeable in these Psalms of meditation. But there are many of them where the throwing of the soul on God in complete confidence becomes the outstanding tone. These are perhaps most frequently used of all the poems of this book.

"The Lord is my shepherd, I shall not want" is the best known hymn of any kind in all the world. Its sublime trust in God is the most complete evidence of the reality of religion to men. But many other Psalms are close rivals of the twenty-third in the beauty of their confidence.

Frequently, these Psalms of trust rise out of the depths of despair. There are the third and fourth that go so well as companions; the one expressing the change of feeling over night with the dawn of the new day, an experience that is common to all those who trust in God; the other expressing the confidence that is found when the troubled heart rests itself in sleep. Thus the third Psalm:

> O Lord, how many are my foes!
>   Many are rising against me;
> many are saying of me,
>   there is no help for him in God.
>
> . . . .
>
> I lie down and sleep;
>   I wake again, for the Lord sustains me.
> I am not afraid of ten thousands of people
>   who have set themselves against me round about.

Here is no reasoning out of the Psalmist's difficulties; only the change of face with a new day of trust. So also the fourth Psalm, of the evening:

> Answer me when I call, O God of my right!
>   Thou hast given me room when I was in distress.
>   Be gracious to me, and hear my prayer.
>
> . . . .
>
> In peace I will both lie down and sleep;
>   for thou alone, O Lord, makest me dwell in safety.

Sometimes the Psalms of trust impress their message with a refrain which the heart loves to sing over and over. Such are the forty-second and forty-third Psalms, which should always be read as one, for they comprise three stanzas of the same poem. They are actually one Psalm in some Bibles, and have evidently been sepa-

rated only by accident in our English Bible. The Psalmist is going into exile and is terror-stricken at the thought of losing contact with
the place where he has been accustomed to worshiping God:

> As a hart longs
>   for flowing streams,
> So longs my soul
>   for thee, O God.
>
> . . . .
>
> When shall I come and behold
>   the face of God?

He feels at times that God has completely forsaken him. "The
land of Jordan" and "Mount Mizar" (42: 6) are the last spots from
which he could view his homeland as he was going into exile to
the northeast, and they have become for him symbols of the "waves
and billows" that have gone over him. Yet ever and again his trust
surges back upon him:

> Oh send out thy light and thy truth;
>   let them lead me,
> let them bring me to thy holy hill
>   and to thy dwelling!

And three times this trust expresses itself, with slight variations,
in the noble refrain:

> Why are you cast down, O my soul,
>   and why are you disquieted within me?
> Hope in God; for I shall again praise him,
>   my help and my God.

The note of trust rising from despair may be observed in many
more Psalms, particularly in the 130th, the "De Profundis" as the
church has long called it. But sometimes this confidence issues
from a contrast between the thought of God as a refuge and any
other shelter. This is most attractively expressed in the beloved 121st
Psalm, which should be read in the Revised Standard Version to get
the point of its question:

> I lift up my eyes to the hills.
>   From whence does my help come?
> My help comes from the Lord,
>   who made heaven and earth.

Psalms of Complaint

Opposite in mood to these hymns of trust are the Psalms of complaint, some of them expressing a dullness of soul that never rises above a weariness with life. Perhaps there are too many times when we tend to share their feeling. Take, for example, the eighty-eighth Psalm. It is often called "The Miserere" because its tone of misery never fades in any of its eighteen verses:

> I am reckoned among those who go down to the Pit;
>   I am a man who has no strength.
>
> . . . .
>
> O Lord, why dost thou cast me off?
>   Why dost thou hide thy face from me?
>
> . . . .
>
> Thou hast caused lover and friend to shun me.

Such a mood of grief, with the feeling that God has brought it on and will not deliver, is fortunately not common in the Psalms. At least not many of them carry it from start to finish as does the eighty-eighth. Yet, in several others it dominates, and even in one of the "Pilgrim Psalms," the 123rd, it abides to the conclusion: ". . . for we have had more than enough of contempt."

Perhaps it should be noted that the expression of complaint is much more common in the Old Testament than in the New. Especially during and after the exile, when men tended to wait for God to bring a long-delayed redemption and when they despaired of having any part in the bringing about of the new age, they tended to develop those habits of mind and heart that led to the wailing wall. The characters of the New Testament, on the other hand, were buoyant with their new-found hope; the kingdom of God was "at hand" and they were actors in the drama of its coming. As we share in one or the other of these quite different points of view, we shall forget all about our complaints in the ecstasy of participation with God, or we shall become dreary and self-concerned. But the Psalms of complaint have at least this good lesson to teach us: if we are bound to be conscious of our ills, we had best bring that consciousness into the presence of God and pour it out there, however bitterly, rather than bottle it up within ourselves or breathe it in some ungodly atmosphere.

Psalms of Earnest Petition

Sometimes the inspired poet can hardly be said to be trusting, nor yet complaining. His mood wavers and is uncertain. But always in such cases there is a pleading seriousness with God, and we may think of them as Psalms of earnest petition. Often the cry is for deliverance from suffering or from sickness or from some enemy, and so the number of Psalms with this emphasis is large.

There are the ninth and tenth for example. They probably do not impress the average reader very much. They belong together both in thought and in form. There is rejoicing in them, but there is also fear mingled with hatred of foes. But the dominant motif seems to be that of beseeching God to take the Psalmist's part:

> Be gracious to me, O Lord!
> Behold what I suffer from those who hate me.
>
> . . . .
>
> Arise, O Lord! Let not man prevail;
> let the nations be judged before thee!
>
> . . . .
>
> Why dost thou stand afar off, O Lord?
> Why dost thou hide thyself in times of trouble?
>
> . . . .
>
> Arise, O Lord; O God, lift up thy hand;
> forget not the afflicted.

These Psalms would be misunderstood if one thought that they meant to teach as a doctrine the idea that the Lord stands "afar off" from the soul that is in trouble. But it is that he so often seems to do just that. It is the feeling of the Psalmist, not the fact of God's action, that constitutes the real theme of such a Psalm.

Even where loving trust breathes through the sacred song, this is sometimes subordinated to the mood of pleading with God. In the thirty-first Psalm, for example, confidence seems to shine as a sun breaking through the clouds, and God seems not as near as the writer could wish:

> My times are in thy hand;
> deliver me from the hand of my enemies and persecutors!

Psalms of Penitence and Forgiveness

Pleading with God reaches its finest point when it is concerned with the forgiveness of sins. This is a common note in many of the Psalms; it is dominant in several of them. Every Christian knows and uses the fifty-first Psalm as the Penitent's heartfelt cry:

> Have mercy on me, O God, according to thy steadfast love;
> according to thy abundant mercy blot out my transgressions.
> Wash me thoroughly from my iniquity,
> and cleanse me from my sin!
> For I know my transgressions,
> and my sin is ever before me.

Whether or not this Psalm was written with the remembrance of David's fearful sin as its background, every heart will respond to its cry for mercy; its sense of dependence on God for cleansing is universal.

But it is not always the tone of anguished pleading that most characterizes these Psalms of the penitent. Sometimes it is the quieter expression of a profound bliss that has resulted from the acceptance of God's forgiveness and the warning of others who may go astray. The thirty-second Psalm contains both of these elements:

> Blessed is he whose transgression is forgiven,
>   whose sin is covered.
>
> . . . .
>
> I will instruct you and teach you
>   the way you should go;
>   I will counsel you with my eye upon you.

Psalms of Thanksgiving

Such a note of joy turns us back to the happier frame of mind and especially to the mood of gratitude. We find many poems in our Psalter that are expressive of thankful remembrance of God's goodness. There is, for example, the buoyant twenty-seventh:

> The Lord is my light and my salvation;
>   whom shall I fear?
> The Lord is the stronghold of my life;
>   of whom shall I be afraid?

This opening paean of trust is followed by a succession of certainties based upon special deliverances from God.

There is the 107th, one of the most remarkably constructed of all the Psalms. It has a general introduction of gratitude:

> O give thanks to the Lord, for he is good;
>   for his steadfast love endures for ever!

The introductory verses (1–3) are followed by a series of stanzas that tell the experiences of people in different walks of life who got into trouble, who sought the Lord in their trouble, and who were delivered. There are the wanderers (vv. 4–9), the prisoners (vv. 10–16), the sick (vv. 17–22), and the sailors at sea (vv. 23–32), each of whom finds special reason for praise. The Psalm is characterized by a double refrain, the first being used after each description of sorrow (vv. 6, 13, 19, 28):

> Then they cried to the Lord in their trouble,
>   and he delivered them from their distress.

The second is a thankful meditation after each deliverance (vv. 8, 15, 21, 31):

> Let them thank the Lord for his steadfast love,
>   for his wonderful works to the sons of men!

Apparently thanksgiving was a rare virtue then as now, and needed urging!

Festal Hymns

These Psalms of thanksgiving for particular blessings, as well as those of adoration of God, strike so universal a response that they have often become enshrined in the memoirs of some special group or indeed of the entire nation. While some of them may have originated as individual songs, many of them seem to have been intended as anthems, celebrating God's coming into his temple in a special manifestation of glory or commemorating the coronation of a king of David's line who was looked upon in a special sense as God's son.

The twenty-fourth Psalm seems to have been meant to be sung by a group of worshipers going up to "the hill of the Lord." It is the praise of a devoted people:

> The earth is the Lord's and the fullness thereof,
>   the world and those who dwell therein.
>
> . . . .
>
> Who shall ascend the hill of the Lord?
>   And who shall stand in his holy place?
> He who has clean hands and a pure heart,
>   who does not lift up his soul to what is false,
>   and does not swear deceitfully.
>
> . . . .
>
> Lift up your heads, O gates!
>   and be lifted up, O ancient doors!
>   that the King of glory may come in.

We can well imagine the pomp and ceremony with which a band of pilgrims, thinking of themselves as God's very own, would enter

Jerusalem with such music. If, as has been suggested, it is probable that this hymn was first written to celebrate the bringing of the ark of God up to its resting place in the holy city, then its festal nature is all the more apparent.

There are several groups of Psalms where any one alone may be thought of as quite personal, but where the group as a whole takes on the festal tone.

Psalms 95–100 form such a group. Separately they classify under the heads of "Adoration" or of "Thanksgiving." They are full of joy and singing. Taken together they breathe the atmosphere of some occasion of celebration, and one suspects that they are grouped in the Psalm Book for such a purpose.

Another such group is 120–134, each called "A Song of Ascent." These fifteen little Psalms are festal in that they constitute the repertoire of pilgrims going up to Jerusalem. Sung at various stopping places or "degrees" of the "ascent" to the religious capital, they seem to have become ritual at an early period of their use. Many of them breathe lamentations over the oppression of God's people, a sentiment which has long characterized Jewish verse.

The best known group of festal hymns is doubtless the "Hallelujah Psalms." Wherever our King James English Bible has the exclamation "Praise ye the Lord," there the Hebrew has the one word "Hallelujah." There are two main groups of these Hallelujah Psalms, 111–117 and 146–150. As individual Psalms they emphasize adoration, but it is well to read them together every now and again that their spirit of exultation may gain with us the momentum it had with God's people of old.

Liturgies

Close akin to these festal Psalms that were sung on occasions is a group that seems not to have been limited to any particular time but that embodies almost all the different elements of worship. We may call them liturgies. Psalm 65 is an excellent example. It begins with praise:

> Praise is due to thee,
>   O God, in Zion;
> and to thee shall vows be performed,
>   O thou who hearest prayer!

The Psalm continues with the note of confession:

> To thee shall all flesh come
>   on account of sins.

The sense of forgiveness follows immediately:

> When our transgressions prevail over us,
>   thou dost forgive them.

And the joy of entrance into God's presence cannot be far behind:

> Blessed is he whom thou dost choose and bring near,
>   to dwell in thy courts!

The note of faith in God waxes strong and amounts almost to a creedal confession:

> By dread deeds thou dost answer us with deliverance,
>   O God of our salvation,
> who art the hope of all the ends of the earth,
>   and of the farthest seas.

Finally the Psalm is turned into an exclamation of praise for the adorable work of God in nature:

> Thou visitest the earth and waterest it,
> . . . .
> Thou crownest the year with thy bounty.

Historical Psalms

The Psalms that have been considered thus far have at least one factor in common: almost all of them seem close to our experience. While they grew no doubt out of specific situations in an ancient environment, they have a timelessness about them that makes them the world's possession.

But the Psalter also contains examples of religious poetry that finds its inspiration, not in universal joys and sorrows, but in peculiarly Hebrew or Jewish settings. The interest that such Psalms have for us lies in the fact that they express the faith that God acted throughout the history of a chosen and covenanted people. If we believe that the Christian church is the covenant people of today, we believe that it is the heritor of that history.

There are Psalms that review in delightful poetic form outstanding moments in the career of Israel. The sixty-eighth, for example, does not dwell on many specific landmarks of history, yet the vivid imagery recalls many an incident of the wilderness wandering:

> Let God arise, let his enemies be scattered;
>   let those who hate him flee before him!
>
> . . . .
>
> the earth quaked, the heavens poured down rain,
>   at the presence of God;
> yon Sinai quaked at the presence of God,
>   the God of Israel.
>
> . . . .
>
> With mighty chariotry, twice ten thousand,
>   thousands upon thousands,
>   the Lord came from Sinai into the holy place.

The numerous shouts of triumph in God that mark the progress of this Psalm have given it the name of "the *Te Deum* of the Hebrews." As is typical in both the Old Testament and the New, very acts of nature are interpreted as the interventions of the Lord on behalf of his people. Thus does the religious faith of the Bible always stress Providence.

Full of particular incidents are such Psalms as the 105th and 106th, where the most casual reader will note the writer's detailed retracing of the wilderness wanderings. The long seventy-eighth seems to be planned to show how all Hebrew history rises to the high-water mark of David's reign. Loveliest of the historical Psalms is the 114th, which, in a few sweeping lines, sets to music the entire Book of Exodus:

When Israel went forth from Egypt,
>   the house of Jacob from a people of strange language,
Judah became his [God's] sanctuary,
>   Israel his dominion.

The sea looked and fled,
>   Jordan turned back.
The mountains skipped like rams,
>   the hills like lambs.

War Psalms

The history of the Israelites, like that of most peoples, was filled with military exploits. Small wonder that their book of national poetry contains some songs of war. The modern reader will perhaps pay less attention to these than to most of the others, though he will not fail to understand their spirit. It is, of course, cheap and easy for a people at war to boast that their cause is righteous; but Israel went further than that in stressing that her God was righteous. There is the twentieth Psalm, which begins with a beautiful benediction and prayer for deliverance:

>   The Lord answer you in the day of trouble!
>   The name of the God of Jacob protect you!
>   May he send you help from the sanctuary,
>   and give you support from Zion!

The Christian does right to lift out of its warlike setting such a stanza of faith and to use it in general devotion. But that it originally had reference to war for which the people were poorly prepared is evident from the way in which it proceeds:

>   May we shout for joy over your victory,
>   and in the name of our God set up our banners!

>   . . . .

>   Some boast of chariots, and some of horses;
>   but we boast of the name of the Lord our God.

The glorification of God's leading in war is more evident still in the twenty-first Psalm, which is companion to the twentieth. Here the Lord is pictured as going forth to fight the nation's battles and to "swallow up" his enemies who have become a "blazing

oven." More direct yet is the claim with which the 144th Psalm
opens:

> Blessed be the Lord, my rock,
> who trains my hands for war,
> and my fingers for battle.

Messianic Psalms

The Psalms that have to do with Israel's history frequently give
expression to the hope in Messiah. As concerned as Christians are
with this hope, we more often go to other books, especially to the
prophets, rather than to the Psalms, for our favorite rendering of
it. Most often in the Psalter Messiah appears as the great military
hero. Thus in the second Psalm:

> The kings of the earth set themselves,
> and the rulers take counsel together,
> against the Lord and against his anointed.
>
> .   .   .   .
>
> He who sits in the heavens laughs;
> the Lord has them in derision.
>
> .   .   .   .
>
> "I have set my king
> on Zion, my holy hill."
>
> .   .   .   .
>
> ". . . Ask of me, and I will make the nations your heritage,
> and the ends of the earth your possession.
> You shall break them with a rod of iron,
> and dash them in pieces like a potter's vessel."

The 110th Psalm gives another picture of a military Messiah:

> "Sit at my right hand,
> till I make your enemies
> your footstool."
>
> .   .   .   .
>
> He will execute judgment among the nations,
> filling them with corpses;
> he will scatter chiefs
> over the wide earth.

There is a sense in which the modern Christian, with the New Testament in hand, fellowships with the note of triumph in such a vision of the Messiah's kingdom, though the picture here drawn of it falls short of the highest revelation to both Hebrews and Christians. God's Spirit will lead us to be more completely sympathetic with the picturing of Messiah as a righteous ruler, such as that of Psalm 72:

> Give the king thy justice, O God,
>   and thy righteousness to the royal son!

Imprecatory Psalms

The Psalms of war and of the warlike character of Israel's expected Messiah often issue in paeans of triumph over defeated foes or in prayer for their undoing. In the midst of acute agony, the Psalmist often invokes the direst curses, or imprecations, on those foes.

The Christian needs to consider carefully the nature of the inspiration of such Psalms. On the one hand, it is not necessary to assume dogmatically that they utter eternal truths that are valid for anyone in any age. But, on the other hand, we too often suppose that we have grown beyond the stage of thought they represent. It is perhaps begging the issue to say that the Psalmist considers himself God's servant, and is therefore invoking wrath upon his enemies because they are God's enemies. The feeling is often too entirely personal to admit of so elevated an explanation. But these Psalms are in the line of inspired literature in this sense, that they give us clear and faithful pictures of the intense feeling of tortured souls, expressed as such souls frequently voice themselves when under direst stress. The feeling may fail of highest worthiness; the expression may leave much for the forgiving Christian to desire; but the "imprecatory Psalms" are, without exception, as honest and as true to life as those historical narratives of the Old Testament which record the sins as well as the virtues of the patriarchs. This honest picture of the depths of torture in the suffering souls of religious men is the real inspiration of these Psalms.

Some of these hymns of condemnation, with fine ethical insight, lay the reason for their imprecation on the moral evil of the enemy. Says the Psalmist of the fifty-eighth:

> The wicked go astray from the womb,
>   they err from their birth, speaking lies.
> They have venom like the venom of a serpent,
>   like the deaf adder that stops its ear.
>
> . . . .
>
> O God, break the teeth in their mouths;
>   tear out the fangs of the young lions, O Lord!

Others of these Psalms throw the emphasis on the suffering through which the Psalmist and his associates have had to pass, and view that as the sufficient reason for bitter prayer. The 137th Psalm expresses this at the greatest extreme:

> By the waters of Babylon,
>   there we sat down and wept,
>   when we remembered Zion.
> On the willows there
>   we hung up our lyres.
> For there our captors
>   required of us songs,
> And our tormentors, mirth, saying,
>   "Sing us one of the songs of Zion!"
>
> . . . .
>
> O daughter of Babylon, you devastator!
>   Happy shall he be who requites you
>   with what you have done to us!
> Happy shall he be who takes your little ones
>   and dashes them against the rock!

No matter what the provocation, it is from this spirit in the Psalms that the Christian will feel himself furthest removed.

Psalms of the Glorification of Zion

It is also to be expected that in a hymnbook of such strong nationalistic feeling, the nation's capital should come in for much

praise. Especially is this true when we reflect that the political center
and the religious center were one. In such use as a Christian may
make of these Psalms, he will, of course, be led to spiritualize them
and to think in terms of his own church, or the religious life of his
own community.

The eighty-seventh Psalm suggests itself as the best example of
this class:

> . . . the Lord loves the gates of Zion
>   more than all the dwelling places of Jacob.
> Glorious things are spoken of you,
>   O city of God.

Psalms of the Law

If Zion was glorified by the Psalmists as Israel's particular rendez-
vous with God, the law was also by at least a few of the Psalmists as
Israel's particular charter.

These Psalms are for the most part well known. The first describes the righteous man as one whose "delight is in the law of the
Lord." The nineteenth is the famous contrast between the law of
the Lord which is "perfect" and the heavens which "are telling the
glory of God." Here the phrases pile up in adulation of the written
testimonies. But in the peculiar 119th, the longest Psalm of all the
book, the praise of the law is drawn out to its furthest reach by the
use of all the synonyms that the Psalmist can think of. Testimonies,
ways, precepts, statutes, commandments, and other terms for the
law crowd into every one of the 176 verses of this monument to
Israel's rule of life.

Psalms of the Future Life

Numbered among these Psalms of more limited interests are a few
that deal with the future life. It is well known that there is very
little in the Old Testament about the life beyond. The Hebrews
were concerned with this present life as "the good." Even those
Psalms that do have something to say about the future will hardly

prove very rewarding to the Christian who has the Gospels and the letters of Paul.

The writers of these Psalms seem not to consider mankind in general as living beyond this life of threescore years and ten. It is the Psalmist's peculiar relation to God that suggests immortality for him. Thus in the forty-ninth Psalm we read,

> Man cannot abide in his pomp,
>   he is like the beasts that perish.
>
> . . . .
>
> But God will ransom my soul from the power of Sheol,
>   for he will receive me.

The writer of the sixteenth Psalm is the most certain of immortality, but definitely limits it to the Messianic person whom he represents as speaking:

> For thou dost not give me up to Sheol,
>   or let thy godly one [a term for Messiah] see the Pit.
>
> Thou dost show me the path of life;
>   in thy presence there is fullness of joy,
>   in thy right hand are pleasures for evermore.

Such "intimations of immortality" were the foundation for the deeper and higher revelation of the New Testament, where not only immortality, but resurrection, and that for all God's faithful, is the glorious hope.

These illustrations of the grouping of the Psalms into sixteen classes can but emphasize the often noted truth that the Psalmists play on every string of the harp of human emotion. The variety and breadth of feeling to be found in the Psalter are perhaps as impressive as its religious faith. It is the acquiring of the deeply worshipful spirit of the book that counts most toward appreciating its permanent worth.

Chapter 6

READING BOOKS TOGETHER

In pursuing the interesting task of finding the units of thought or of feeling in the Bible, the reader is bound to discover that a number of them are repeated or closely paralleled, either in the same book or in a similar book. Isaiah's beautiful passage on peace, for example, is practically identical with Micah's: Isaiah 2: 2–4 and Micah 4: 1–3. Psalms 14 and 53 are so nearly alike that anyone can tell they are the same composition preserved in two places. Psalm 18 is to be found again in the twenty-second chapter of II Samuel. The fact that a Psalm may have been used sometimes as a single hymn of worship and at other times as part of the longer liturgy we were illustrating in the last chapter is to be seen in the recurrence of the seventieth Psalm as the last part of the fortieth. Some of the stories about Jesus and a number of his best known teachings are nearly word for word in two and sometimes in three Gospels. There are the parables associated with the question about fasting which are nearly identical in Matt. 9: 14–17, Mark 2: 18–22, and Luke 5: 33–39. There is Jesus' teaching on the disciples' cross: Matt. 16: 24–28, Mark 8: 34–9: 1, and Luke 9: 23–27. Or there is the telling tale of Jesus' unanswerable question, given in reply to the challenge of his authority: Matt. 21: 23–27, Mark 11: 27–33, and Luke 20: 1–8.

Most such passages, it will be noted, are brief. Exact correspondences are seldom numerous enough, except in the first three Gospels, to warrant a special endeavor to read them together. But there

58

are many ways in which longer passages, indeed whole books of the Bible, suggest one another. To find these large-scale comparisons and to parallel them in one's reading is often to vivify the meaning.

BOOKS THAT DEAL WITH THE SAME TIMES

It is a good departure from the ordinary methods of Bible reading to take together books that deal with the same period of history. This does not necessarily mean that these books were written at the same time, but that they concern themselves with contemporary events. The book of Judges, for instance, is traditionally very old. No one knows just when the little book of Ruth was written. Many feel that it was probably composed late in Jewish history, at a time of the preaching of the missionary spirit. But the book of Ruth deals with the days of the judges. Not that any of the story of Ruth is told in the book of Judges itself, but that its whole background is in the longer book. To read Ruth along with Judges is to note many similarities in living conditions, in customs of society, in physical and moral dangers, even in ideals. The atmosphere of the book of Ruth justifies its opening sentence: "In the days when the judges ruled there was a famine in the land."

But there are other writings dealing with the same times that do have very closely related materials. The books of Kings and Chronicles have much in common. To be sure, the Chronicles were written long after the books of the Kings. The earlier writing was done when the prophets of Israel were just coming into their own, and so the books of Kings view the history of the united kingdom and then of the divided kingdom, largely from the standpoint of the prophets' interpretation of religion. The Chronicles, compiled after the exile, at a time when the rule was largely in the hands of the priests, tend to interpret the same history in terms of the good and bad in worship. Moreover, the chronicler goes clear back to Adam for his beginning and brings his story down to date, while the earlier historian starts with the death of David (where the books of Samuel left off) and ends with the capture of Jerusalem. And yet again, the books of the Kings lay the stress on the northern kingdom, after the division under Solomon's son, for the northern kingdom was the larger of the two and the more important commercially and politically. But the books of the Chronicles highlight the southern kingdom, true as it always remained to the line of David, with its temple worship and its sacrificial system developing constantly. Nevertheless, these very differences make it all the more interesting to read these books together. To get the two stories of Solomon's reign, to follow especially such Judaean kings as Jehoshaphat, Joash, Hezekiah, and Josiah from the two standpoints, is to see the basic principles in these men's characters that persist through the ages, as well as the changes in thought about certain of their deeds which later reflection brought about. Seldom has it been considered worth while to publish a "harmony" of Kings and Chronicles, but a way of interweaving the two is suggested in chapter 7.

It has long been the custom to read the Gospels as one as well as four. Harmonies with parallel columns, showing the stories that are told in two, three, or all four of them, are known to most readers of the Bible; but it is very hard to fit the stories of the Gospel of John into the framework of the first three with any degree of certainty in chronological arrangement. In our general outlines in chapter 8 will be found, not the actual printing of the biblical text of course, but units of parallel reading, so that even if one does not possess a separate "Harmony of the Gospels," he may read the four profitably together.

Often close readers have gone further than this with the Gospels, and have read them even more truly as one, omitting repeated passages and choosing in each case the longest or most vivid telling of a story that occurs in more than one of them. As early as the second century, a Syrian Christian by the name of Tatian published what he called "The Diatessaron," which means, "through the four," a work in which he went through the four Gospels in this fashion, giving the actual New Testament text, but using any given story of the Gospels only once.

BOOKS OF TEACHING
THAT GO WITH BOOKS OF HISTORY

Not only two or more historical books that deal with the same times may well be read together, but often passages of teaching are much more clearly understood if they are read along with the books that relate the story of the times in which their teaching arose.

This is one of the most profitable ways in which to come to know many of the prophets. Usually one will find in the very first verse of a prophet's book some historical note. As a rule this will list the names of the kings under whose rule the prophet labored. Now if the reader will turn back to the books of Kings (or Chronicles), find the story of the times of these particular kings, and read it as a background for the prophecies, he will often find an illuminating commentary. Thus, at the opening of the book of Isaiah, we read: "The vision of Isaiah the son of Amoz, which he saw concerning Judah and Jerusalem, in the days of Uzziah, Jotham, Ahaz, and Hezekiah, kings of Judah." Here we at once realize that we are dealing only with the southern kingdom of Judah. We turn back to II Kings 15, 16, and 18–20, and find the stories of these kings, omitting the 17th chapter if we like because it deals with a rule in northern Israel. We shall even find the name of Isaiah in these passages linked with the history of the times. The parallel passages in II Chronicles 26–32 are even more detailed, especially at the point of the great faith of Hezekiah.

Similarly, the prophecy of Amos notes that the word of the Lord came to the prophet "in the days of Uzziah king of Judah, and in the days of Jeroboam the son of Joash, king of Israel." So we shall want to turn to the historical note at the end of chapter 14 in II Kings as well as the whole of chapter 15. All the kings of the times of Isaiah and Amos are represented in the historical word at the opening of the prophecy of Hosea, and we have a rather complete background of the two kingdoms in the wonderful pictures he paints. The book of Jeremiah takes us to a later time, notifying us at its outset that the word of the Lord came to Jeremiah in the

reigns of Josiah, Jehoiakim, and Zedekiah. Hence we shall do well
to refresh our memories of these times with the closing chapters of
II Kings, 22–25. Some of the prophets are, indeed, undated, but
wherever their flaming oracles can be seen in the light of the history
of a particular period, an added light will be given.

Similarly, in the New Testament, the letters of Paul will be much
more enjoyed if they are read in connection with the parts of the
book of Acts that tell us of Paul's activities in the cities to which
the letters were addressed. Thus, if one reads the story of the Jerusalem conference in Acts 15 and the account of Paul's visit to the
Galatian towns in chapter 16, he will be prepared for the spirit of
debate and the struggles of Jewish and Gentile forces which the
letter to the Galatians magnifies. If one reads the 17th chapter of
Acts with its story of persecution in Thessalonica, and then follows
it with Paul's two letters to the Thessalonians, he will be more
sympathetic with the apostle's handling of persecution and trouble.
If he reads the account of the long stay at Corinth, in the 18th chapter of Acts, especially after the history of the disappointment at
Athens that has just preceded, he will be ready to follow the ups
and downs of the church problems which Paul meets in his two
letters to the Corinthians. Much of the common impression that
the apostle Paul is cold or hard to understand could be cleared up by
thus linking his writings with the history of the occasions for them.

BOOKS OF SIMILAR THEMES

Often one of these books of teachings can be read advantageously
with another of its kind. The prophecies of Amos and Hosea, noted
above, are not only from the same general period, but they deal in
similar realism with the sins of Israel and of Judah in the eighth
century before Christ. If one adds to them their later contemporary,
Micah, he has a group of three whose subject matter is remarkably
akin in many respects, yet who supplement each other in such a way
as to impress the reader with the many-sidedness of the religion of
faith. Or Micah may well be read with the first part of Isaiah, for

both prophets spoke mainly to the southern kingdom of Judah, and at the same time. We have already noted the passage on peace that occurs in both. The reader will find much of the same religious zeal and many of the same expressions of truth in the rustic Micah and the urban Isaiah. Joel and Zephaniah both deal with "the day of the Lord," and may well be read together. Haggai and the first part of Zechariah are interesting parallels of preaching to the returned exiles in an effort to stir them up to rebuild their ruined temple—an effort which succeeded. The book of Ecclesiastes includes many words of wisdom that are comparable to those in the Proverbs.

When we turn to the New Testament the parallelism of subject matter is even more frequent. Not only in the Gospels, where the life of Christ is, of course, the common theme, but in many of the letters group reading will uncover repeated thoughts. Thus Paul's dealing with the law and faith in the third and fourth chapters of his Letter to the Galatians finds a close parallel in the same chapters of Romans. His Letters to the Ephesians and to the Colossians are constructed on the same plan. In each case the first half of the letter deals with the apostle's teaching on the person of Christ and on the church. In each case also, the second half deals with the applications of the principles of Christian living, especially in the home. Many Christians have noted the repeated instructions which these writings afford concerning the relation of husbands and wives, parents and children, masters and servants. Again in Paul's pastorals there is a close parallel between I Timothy and Titus in his view of the church and especially of desirable qualifications for church officers.

But other apostles besides Paul exhibit this frequent similarity of thought. No one can read the Gospel of John, and then follow it with the three Letters of John, without being struck with the repetition of the same few teachings, in the expression of which the same few simple words are used again and again. To mention truth, love, light, Father, children, will, Spirit, is to note John's peculiar emphasis.

Nor is it always the same apostle who gives us parallel themes in different parts of his writings. The similarity of James with the

Gospel of Matthew, particularly with the Sermon on the Mount,
has often been pointed out. And no reader of the Bible can fail to
note that he is reading twice almost the same tirade against false
teachers in the church when he follows Jude with the Second Letter
of Peter.

Contrasting Uses of the Same Themes

Truth often glows by contrast as well as by comparison. So one
may also find in the Bible numerous instances of books that may
well be read together to get a view of quite different ways of dealing
with the same subject. Some of these books which we have men-
tioned as being quite comparable also contain examples of notable
contrasts. This is true of any two of the Gospels, for the strange
thing about them is not only that they are so much alike in many
particulars, but that they are so different in others. We may instance
the handling of the story of John the Baptist by Matthew or Mark,
and its very different handling by John. A similar thing is true of
Kings and Chronicles. With all their parallels they exhibit many
variant ways of treating the same incident. Witness the story of
David numbering the people, told in Kings as a temptation of God
and in Chronicles as a temptation of Satan. These accounts are not
contradictory, as is sometimes supposed, but rather they are evidence of the growth of God's revelation of himself to Israel. In the
early days when Kings was written, God was thought of as the direct
cause of everything that happened. All was in some way his will. By
the days of the Chronicles the people had learned that some things
happen in opposition to God's will.

There are still better examples of contrasts in dealing with themes
in books that we have not cited as being similar. Joshua and Judges
will naturally be read together because the one is followed by the
other in our Bibles. This is well, for the book of Joshua tells the
story of the conquest of Canaan from the idealistic standpoint of
the plan and purpose of God, while Judges tells it from the realistic
view of how much of that plan was left unfinished. Nahum voices

the doom which God has pronounced on Nineveh, while the book of Jonah tells the tale of the pain by which the prophet discovered God's love for Nineveh.

These contrasts are to be seen at their most significant stage when we read together a book from the Old Testament and another from the New. Thus, if the reader who has waded through the accounts of the offerings and sacrifices in the book of Leviticus and has learned to relish its description of priests and days of atonement will turn at once to the book of Hebrews, he will find priest and offering, atonement, and covenant treated from the new Christian vantage point of the superiority of Jesus to all the forms of the old dispensation. If the reader of the law with its humanitarian emphasis in Deuteronomy will turn to Paul's Letter to the Galatians, he will find law dealt with as a preparation for the gospel of faith. There is much of the Old Testament in the New, but the Old is often as milk for children, while the New is as strong meat for the mature.

TABLE OF COMBINATIONS OF BOOKS

The following may serve as a suggestive summary of the thought of this chapter by illustrating a number of combinations of Old and New Testament books or parts of books that will be likely to have new meaning when read consecutively.

1. *Old Testament Books*

   a. Exodus, Leviticus, Numbers—for something of a connected story of Israel's wilderness experience.
   b. Deuteronomy and Joshua—for the contrast and comparison of the two leaderships of Moses and Joshua.
   c. Joshua and Judges—for the contrast of the two accounts of settlement in Canaan.
   d. Judges and Ruth—since the scene of Ruth is laid in the days of the judges.
   e. Ruth and Esther—the two heroine books of the Old Testament.
   f. Samuel and Kings—for the connected story of Israel's monarchy.

g. Kings and Chronicles—for the contrast of an earlier with a later interpretation of the monarchy.

h. Ezra and Nehemiah—for related history of the days following the return from captivity.

i. Psalms and Proverbs—for the poetry and proverbs of each.

j. Proverbs and Ecclesiastes—for the proverbial or "wisdom" type of literature in each.

k. Isaiah and Micah—contemporary prophets to Judah.

l. Jeremiah and Ezekiel—prophets of the exile.

m. Hosea and Amos—contemporary prophets of northern Israel.

n. Amos, Hosea, and Micah (in this order)—for the growth of prophecy in the 8th century b.c., the "classic age" of Israel's prophets.

o. Obadiah, Jonah, and Nahum—prophecies against foreign peoples.

p. Joel and Zephaniah—two prophets of "the day of the Lord."

q. Jeremiah and Habakkuk—seventh century prophets who faced doubts.

r. Haggai and Zechariah—prophets of the rebuilding of the temple.

2. *New Testament Books*

a. Matthew, Mark, and Luke—for the "Synoptic" picture of the ministry of Jesus.

b. Matthew and Luke—for the similarity of teaching material.

c. Matthew and John—for two argumentative styles.

d. The Gospel of John and the Letters of John—for close similarity of thought and figures of speech.

e. Luke and Acts—for one writer's connected story of Christ and his church.

f. Acts and the Pauline Letters—for the early history of the church.

g. Romans and Galatians—for their similar treatment of faith and law.

h. Ephesians and Colossians—for their similar treatment of the headship of Christ.

i. I and II Thessalonians—for a misunderstanding and its correction.

j. I Timothy and Titus—for similar dealing with church organization.

    k. Philippians and II Timothy—for contrasting pictures of Paul as a prisoner.

    l. Philippians and Philemon—two pictures of Paul's tenderer side.

    m. Hebrews and I Peter—two letters dealing with the Christian attitude toward suffering and persecution.

    n. II Peter and Jude—two very similar letters about false teachers.

3. *Books of Both Testaments*

    a. Leviticus, Chronicles, and Hebrews—for the Bible's emphasis on the priest.

    b. Deuteronomy, Galatians, and Romans—for contrasts and comparisons in the treatment of law.

    c. Proverbs and James—for the "wisdom literature" of each.

    d. Isaiah 7–11, 40–53, Malachi, and Matthew—for prophecy and its realization in Jesus Christ.

    e. Amos and Romans—for the emphasis on the righteousness of God.

    f. Hosea and John—for the emphasis on the love of God.

    g. Daniel and Revelation—for the two best illustrations of the use of Apocalypse in the Bible, a use which will be explained in chapter 11.

Chapter 7

UNITS OF READING
IN THE OLD TESTAMENT

"The proof of the pudding is the eating thereof." We come now to apply to the actual reading of the Bible the suggestions offered in the preceding chapters.

Immediately we are faced with one real perplexity. What shall be our attitude toward the Old Testament? It is three times the length of the New Testament. Shall we proceed at approximately the same rate, dividing it into units of about the same reading time? That practice has tended to overemphasize the Old Testament in the mind of the church. Because we have put all of the Bible on very much the same plane, our theology and our church practices have been overweighted with the thought and language of the Old Testament. This is a vital error, for we are New Testament Christians, and the interpretation of Jesus Christ which the New Testament contains is our immediate basis of faith.

But shall we, on the other hand, slight or even ignore the Old Testament? Shall we think of it as outmoded? The anti-Semitic propaganda of Central Europe went further than this. It sought to root out of men's thinking the religious patterns of the ancient Hebrews. It undertook to do what the heretic Marcion attempted in the early days of the church—to reform even our New Testament so as to cut from it the influence of the Old.

Yet the New Testament is simply filled with the Old. Quotations, direct and indirect, references, allusions, meet the eye on every page. To read the New Testament without the Old would be first

68

to rewrite the New Testament. To try to follow the New without the background of the Old would be to render it almost meaningless at many important places. More important than this: the theology of the New Testament is steeped in that of the Old. Such basic teachings as those of the righteousness of God, his love, his covenant for his people, his judgment and mercy, his oneness and holiness, reappear in our New Testament much as they have been formulated in the Old. Even the teachings that seem completely original in the New Testament, such as the trinity, the cross, and the resurrection, have forerunners in suggestions and longings of the Old that peer out here and there, as it were, from behind drawn curtains.

We are faced then with the desirability of "putting the Old Testament in its place" in our reading—a place of honor and of recognition of permanent worth, but a place that is not proportionate to its length. The relatively long historical narratives of ancient Israel teem with understanding of the meaning of life with God. The devotional books give rest to the weary hearts of all generations. The prophets speak with fire from off an eternal altar. Yet the Old ever falls short of the unveiling of the face of God which the New turns out to be.

Perhaps the best way to meet this dual difficulty is to read the Old Testament by its natural units of division as we shall attempt to do with the New, but to group the shorter units of the Old in larger units wherever that is possible and so read more rapidly. It has already been intimated in chapters 2 and 3 that reading large amounts at a time is desirable. This is especially true in the case of the Old Testament. In the following outlines of books, we shall suggest these larger units by figures. Wherever the larger units can be appropriately divided into shorter ones for those who feel they must go more slowly, we shall represent the latter by letters. Reading should be done, whenever possible, in the longer portions to get the best results. These are the real units of thought. It would be better to read from the Bible only two or three times a week, than to nibble at a little something each day just to be able to say, "I haven't let a day go by without reading the Bible."

GENESIS: UNITS OF OUTSTANDING CHARACTERS

In chapter 4 we have used the book of Genesis as an illustration of "Story Units of Characters." This may well be reread before taking Genesis straight through. We may arrange the book as follows in longer and shorter units:

1. The story of creation. Chs. 1, 2.
    a. From the standpoint of God's orderly work. 1: 1–2: 3.
    b. From the standpoint of God's purpose for man. 2: 4–25.
2. Sin and judgment of mankind: the unit of Adam. Chs. 3–5.
    (Ch. 5 is a listing of the patriarchs, but vv. 21–32 contain many significant side lights.)
3. Righteousness and unrighteousness: the unit of Noah. 6: 1–11: 25.
    (The lists of Noah's descendants, ch. 10, may be omitted, also the abbreviated genealogy of Abraham, 11: 10–25).
4. The righteousness that is by faith: the unit of Abram (Abraham). 11: 26–25: 18.
    a. The wanderer, guided by God. 11: 26–16: 16.
    b. The struggle of faith and unrighteousness. Chs. 17–20.
    c. The victory of righteous faith. Chs. 21, 22.
    d. Abraham's old age. 23: 1–25: 18.
5. God's transforming power: the unit of Jacob. 25: 19–37: 1.
    a. In the home of Isaac. 25: 19–27: 46.
    b. Flight and foreign residence. Chs. 28–30.
    c. Return. 31: 1–37: 1.
    (Ch. 36, the lists of the descendants of Esau, may be omitted.)
6. The working out of God's purpose: the unit of Joseph. 37: 2–50: 26.
    a. Innocence and debauchery. Chs. 37, 38.
    b. From dungeon to service in high places. Chs. 39–41.
    c. On being a brother. 42: 1–45: 15.
    d. Restored relations of Joseph and his father. 45: 16–48: 22.
    e. The last days of Jacob and Joseph. Chs. 49, 50.

EXODUS: UNITS OF EPOCHAL EVENTS

The book of Exodus cannot, like Genesis, be divided into units of outstanding characters. There is but one character of any moment in Exodus, and that is Moses. But the book contains the history of some of the most formative of Israel's experiences. Here is the story of the learning of the name of Israel's redemptive God in Moses' contact at the burning bush. Here is the careful explanation of the institution of the Passover, first and greatest of Israel's feasts. And here is the dramatic recital of the giving of the Law, Israel's basic charter. The book of Exodus is among the most important of the Old Testament.

1. The preparation of Moses for leadership. Chs. 1-4.
2. The struggle with Pharaoh. 5: 1-15: 21.
   a. Early experiences at court. 5: 1-7: 13.
   b. Nine plagues fail to move Pharaoh. 7: 14-10: 29.
   c. The Passover and the exodus from Egypt at the death of the first-born. 11: 1-15: 21.
3. The giving of the moral law. 15: 22-20: 26.
4. The giving of ordinances of worship: the law of holiness. Chs. 21-24.
5. The tabernacle planned. Chs. 25-31.
   (This may be skipped through hastily, as its details scarcely affect our religious interests.)
6. Sin and the renewal of favor. 32: 1-35: 3.
7. The tabernacle completed. 35: 4-40: 38.
   (Again the details may be scanned, but ch. 40 should be read carefully.)

LEVITICUS: UNITS OF LAW

The book of Leviticus does not have the interest for us as Christians that is to be found in Genesis and Exodus. As has been noted in chapter 6, it offers a good background for the understanding of the Letter to the Hebrews. The very wearisomeness of some of its detail of offerings and of its meticulous laws of clean and unclean impresses us with the need for the new covenant not written in ordinances which the book of Hebrews glorifies.

Leviticus contains, however, an elaborate account of the Day of Atonement (ch. 16) which should be carefully studied by every Christian.

The following larger units are probably too long for reading at one sitting, because of their monotony if for no other reason. On the other hand, the shorter units into which Unit 4 is divided, while necessarily short if the several subjects treated here are to be recognized, should be read at least two at a time.

1. Laws of offerings. Chs. 1–7. (May be broken, if necessary, at any recurrence of the phrase, "The Lord said to Moses.")
2. Laws of priesthood. Chs. 8–10.
3. Laws of clean and unclean. Chs.11–15.
   (May be skimmed to see the various illustrations. Careful reading is hardly necessary.)
4. Laws of holiness. Chs. 16–27.
   a. National holiness and the Day of Atonement. Ch. 16.
   b. Personal holiness. Chs. 17–21.
   c. Holiness of feasts and offerings. Chs. 22–24.
   d. The holiness of land. Ch. 25.
   e. Blessings on the devoted. Ch. 26.
   f. The holiness of vows and dues. Ch. 27.

Numbers: Units of Wanderings

The book of Numbers illustrates clearly the point of view of these outlines, that the Old Testament should be read by the Christian with discrimination, not missing points of vital interest, yet not wasting time on tribal records that mean next to nothing to us. Unit 1 contains little of concern. Unit 2 is far more interesting, save for shorter unit c. Under unit 3, shorter unit a is important, while the remainder is mostly chronicle. The division of the entire book by significant stopping places in the desert wanderings of the children of Israel suggests itself readily. The book takes its name from the two numberings which it records.

1. Sinai still the center. 1: 1–10: 10.
   a. Taking the first census. Chs. 1–4. (Skimmed.)
   b. Various laws and gifts. 5: 1–10: 10.
      (The delight in the piling up of repetition in a story reaches its height in ch. 7.)
2. The journey through the desert. 10: 11–21: 35.
   a. The journey to Paran. 10: 11–12: 16.

    b. The sending of the spies. Chs. 13, 14.
    c. Miscellaneous laws and events. Chs. 15–19.
    d. The last of the desert. Chs. 20, 21.
3. On the steppes of Moab. Chs. 22–36.
    a. The story of Balaam. Chs. 22–24.
    b. Events surrounding the second census. Chs. 25–27.
    c. New and old in regulations. Chs. 28–36.
       (To be sketched hastily.)

DEUTERONOMY: UNITS OF PUBLIC ADDRESS

The word "Deuteronomy" means "the second law." The book contains a second giving of the law in the sense that it records several of Moses' last addresses to the children of Israel on the steppes of Moab where the book of Numbers left them. These addresses do contain many particular laws repeated from the preceding three books. Deuteronomy is far from mere repetition, however. It is new interpretation. It is significant classification of laws. It is a humanitarian explanation of law that is worthy of the finest mind and heart. Its careful assigning of reason for law appeals to the fair-mindedness of men. Thus the recording of the commandments by Moses in Deuteronomy 5 is really more meaningful for the Christian than the better known code of Exodus 20. And what is perhaps more important still, the book of Deuteronomy does full justice to the magnificence of the character of Moses in this noble portrayal of his spoken rhetoric. Most scholars consider it to have been the "book of the law" found in the temple in the days of King Josiah's reforms (II Kings, chs. 22, 23).

To divide the book for reading at the points of the beginnings of Moses' addresses is of course to undertake quite unequal units. The second address is longer than the others taken together. But with the suggestion of shorter units for further division, especially of this second address, the plan commends itself as the most natural.

1. The address of retrospect. 1: 1–4: 43.
2. The spiritual interpretation of the law. 4: 44–26: 19.

   a. The law of the new covenant. 4: 44–11: 32.
       (This will seem rather long for one reading, but its fine flow
       should not be broken if possible. Division at ch. 9 is least ob-
       jectionable, since before this the emphasis is on the holy law and
       the holy people, while from ch. 9 on the stress is on obedience.)
   b. The uncodified law. Chs. 12–26.
       (This reading may be conveniently broken at any chapter.)
3. The blessing and the curse. Chs. 27–30.
   a. Curse and warning. Chs. 27, 28.
   b. Terms of the covenant of blessing. Chs. 29, 30.
4. Moses' farewell and death. Chs. 31–34.
   a. Commission and song. Chs. 31, 32.
   b. Final blessing and death. Chs. 33, 34.

Joshua: Units of Conquest

The book of Joshua gives the story of that leader's ideal conquest
of Palestine and of his division of it among the tribes. Not that the
land stayed conquered in the way this narrative describes. The suc-
ceeding book of the Judges makes that clear. Nor that all the land
was ever possessed according to the methodical lines that Joshua
measured off. Rather the book is to be looked upon as presenting a
first hurried invasion with a setting of an ideal standard for oc-
cupancy. Aside from some of its interesting stories of stratagem, the
rest of the book will be passed over as hurriedly by the Christian as
the Israelites passed over the land of promise. The testing of the
people's faith and morals at Jericho and Ai will strike familiar chords
for most readers.

1. Strategies of conquest. Chs. 1–12.
   a. Crossing the Jordan. Chs. 1–4.
   b. The conquest of the north. Chs. 5–9.
   c. The conquest of the south. Chs. 10–12.
2. Division of the land among the tribes. Chs. 13–22.
       (To be skipped through, save for the first part of ch. 18 and all of
       ch. 22.)
3. Joshua's farewell. Chs. 23, 24.

JUDGES: UNITS OF LEADERSHIP

The book of Judges presents the sad story of the Israelites' failure "to possess their possessions." It is the collection of Hebrew wild west stories, the tale of days of no central authority that lay between the organization under Joshua and that under Samuel. "Every man did what was right in his own eyes." This repeated statement of the book (17:6; 21:25) strikes us with terror as we read the evidence of barbarity. Superstition, selfishness, sensuality rule the families and tribes of Israel. Enemies from all quarters infest the hills and plains.

In such days the "judges" were not judicial experts in our sense of the term. They were rather military deliverers, rescuing one or more tribes at a time from some neighboring enemy, and being accorded the right to hear disputes between Israelites as a result. The units of reading in the book are obviously the points at which principal leaders appear. In a sense this book, like Genesis, contains units of character, though in this case the individual is of far less importance and the national significance looms larger.

1. The failure of the Israelites to inherit Palestine: early judges. Chs. 1-3.
2. Deborah, and the need of "a mother in Israel." Chs. 4, 5.
3. Gideon, and the need of a central power. Chs. 6-9.
   a. The work of Gideon. 6: 1-8: 28.
   b. The decadence of Gideon's family. 8: 29-9: 57.
4. Jephthah, and trouble from across Jordan. Chs. 10-12.
5. Samson, and the Philistine raids. Chs. 13-16.
6. Typical crimes of the day. Chs. 17-21.
   a. The story of Micah and the Danites. Chs. 17, 18.
   b. The story of Gibeah and the Benjamites. Chs. 19-21.

RUTH: A STORY UNIT

It has already been pointed out in chapter 3 that to read this little book in any other way than at one sitting is to miss much of the loveliness of its contribution to the redeeming side of the days of the judges. Its chief purpose in the Old Testament canon is to counteract any feeling of pride that Israel had developed in being a "peculiar people." To do this the writer has directed the entire story toward the climax (4: 13–22) where he has made it clear that Ruth, a Moabitess and hence a non-Hebrew, became in a few generations the ancestress of King David himself. Thus the ecumenical note of God's concern for all peoples, which we have observed in such poems as Psalms 67 and 100, embraces even the doctrine of the covenant.

I Samuel: Units of Leadership

Our two books of Samuel were originally one, covering about a century of Israel's history. During this time the scattered tribes were welded into a nation. The books do not contain a dry narration of events, but a prophetic interpretation of the way God worked to bring about the unity of his people. It was not so much their common customs as their faith that made of them a single people.

I Samuel is built around the leadership of three men, Samuel, Saul, and David, the first of them giving his name to the work. For it was Samuel who broke up the old round of the dominance of some "judge" over one or more tribes and who called the people to a united service of God as king. But it was also Samuel who grieved that the people wanted an earthly king in order to be like their neighbors. He finally consented, but insisted that a human king could be only the representative of the divine, and he warned the people that such a king would inevitably establish a military sway that would conscript their sons from lives of freedom and would raise taxes to huge proportions. Both books of Samuel are amazingly honest in portraying, not only the strong features, but the failures and gross sins of their national leaders.

1. Samuel outstanding. Chs. 1–8.
   a. Childhood and rise of Samuel. Chs. 1–3.
   b. Philistine wars. 4: 1–7: 14.
   c. Samuel's dilemma. 7: 15–8: 22.

2. Saul outstanding. Chs. 9–15.
  a. The choice of Saul. Chs. 9–12.
  b. Saul's jealousy. Chs. 18–20.
3. David outstanding. Chs. 16–31.
  a. The rise of David. Chs. 16, 17.
  b. Saul's jealousy. Chs. 18–20.
  c. David in flight from Saul. Chs. 21–24.
  d. Outlaw experiences of David. 25: 1–28: 2.
  e. The end of Saul. 28: 3–31: 13.

II Samuel: Units of Moral Effects of Character

The second book of Samuel should be ranked among the outstanding pieces of the world's literature from the standpoint of its ability to portray the relation between the moral character of leaders and the results in the fortunes of their people. The first part of the book paints the good side of David's character with the triumphs, spiritual and temporal, that ensue. The latter half is a vivid moving picture of demoralization in the family of David, all of it traceable to David's own moral collapse.

A. The good side: David's early reign, and the triumph of virtue. Chs. 1–10.
  1. David's kindness to the house of Saul. Chs. 1–4.
  2. David recovers Israel religiously. Chs. 5–7.
  3. David recovers Israel politically. Chs. 8–10.
B. The bad side: David's family troubles the result of sin. Chs. 11–24.
  4. David's sin. Chs. 11, 12.
  5. Domestic troubles. Chs. 13, 14.
  6. Absalom's revolt. Chs. 15–20.
     (An effectively told story that should be read, if possible, as the single unit that it is.)
    a. "Stealing the hearts" of the people. Chs. 15–17.
    b. The fearfulness of civil war. 18: 1–19: 8.
    c. David's recovery of power. 19: 9–20: 25.
  7. The last years of David's reign. Chs. 21–24.
     (Chs. 21 and 23 consist in part of lists of heroes that may be skipped.)

I Kings: Units of Kingdom Fortunes

On the surface the books of the Kings tell the story of the spread of the Hebrew kingdom to its farthest extent under Solomon, of its disruption at his death, and of the varying fortunes of the northern and southern divisions of that kingdom until the fall of each. Units of reading may be appropriately grouped around the tales of these shifting fortunes. But in a more profound sense these books interpret the struggle that continued for some four hundred years between those who sought to harmonize the culture of Israel with the more developed civilization into the midst of which the people had come and those who, on the other hand, endeavored to keep pure the covenant allegiance to Israel's God.

1. Solomon and the united kingdom. Chs. 1–11.
   a. The rise of Solomon. Chs. 1, 2.
   b. The character of Solomon. Chs. 3, 4.
   c. The temple built and dedicated. 5: 1–9: 9.
      (Chs. 6 and 7, containing details of the temple, may be omitted or skimmed through.)
   d. Solomon's tricks and sins. 9: 10–11: 43.
2. The early days of the divided kingdom. 12: 1–16: 20.
   a. Jeroboam's policies of separatism. 12: 1–14: 20.
   b. Wars between the two kingdoms. 14: 21–16: 20.
3. Omri and the policy of syncretism. 16: 21–22: 53.
   a. Religion and the prophets. 16: 21–19: 21.
   b. The internal policies of Ahab. Chs. 20, 21.
   c. The foreign policy of Ahab. Ch. 22.

II Kings: Units of Kingdom Fortunes
(Continued)

1. Israel and Judah in league. Chs. 1–8.
   a. The new order. Chs. 1–3.
   b. The deeds of the great Elisha. Chs. 4–8.
      (May be broken either at ch. 5 or ch. 6, but much more effective if read as a unit.)
2. Jehu's anti-Baal revolution and the policy of the enforced worship of God. Chs. 9–11.

3. Political weaknesses following revolution. Chs. 12–17.
    a. Decadent royalty. 12: 1–15: 7.
    b. Revolts and the fall of Samaria. 15: 8–17: 41.
4. Judah's faithful Hezekiah. Chs. 18–20.
5. Reaction and reform. 21: 1–23: 30.
6. Judah's decline and fall. 23: 31–25: 30.

I CHRONICLES: UNITS OF THE RELIGIOUS SIGNIFICANCE OF HISTORY

The books of the Chronicles cover much of the same material as II Samuel and the books of Kings. As has already been pointed out in chapter 6, in connection with reading books together, the point of view of Kings is that of the prophets, while the point of view of Chronicles is that of the post-exilic priests in whose days the Chronicles were drawn up. The books of Chronicles look back upon the history of God's chosen from the vantage point of several centuries, and so they tend to idealize. This does not mean that they are untrue to history, but that they select the best in the history and bring it to the front. This is especially true in their handling of the fortunes of the divided kingdom. As the priests look back upon the days before the exile, they feel that the southern kingdom of Judah, which always remained true to the house of David, had the really religious contribution to make. This is stressed at times by simply passing over the bad side of Judah's history. Thus, in contrast to the prominent notation in II Samuel of the good and the bad sides of David's character, it is readily observed that the Chronicles almost ignore any bad in David.

The units of reading properly suggest what we have called above "the religious significance of history." This stress on religion finds its expression in an emphasis on worship, on the construction of the temple, the organization of choirs and the singing of psalms and hymns, and especially on the functions of the priests.

The books open with nine chapters of genealogical tables, so dear to the hearts of the hunters for "pure blood" which the priests of the days after the exile surely were.

1. Genealogies of the Jews. Chs. 1–9.
     (To be omitted in reading, save to note such worthy comments
     as: 1: 10; 4: 9, 10; 5: 20–22; 6: 32; 9: 21–34.
2. David's religious reign. Chs. 10–29.
   a. The rise of David. Chs. 10–12.
   b. The religion of David. Chs. 13–17.
   c. David's victories and losses. Chs. 18–21.
   d. David organizes worship and public defense for entrusting to
      Solomon. Chs. 22–29.
      (Omit chs. 24–27, lists of officers, etc.)

II Chronicles: Units of the Religious Significance of History (Continued)

The second book of the Chronicles reminds one in some respects
of the book of Judges. Outstandingly religious kings of the southern
kingdom of Judah are selected for prominent treatment because
they were deliverers of their people at critical junctures.

1. The glorious reign of Solomon. Chs. 1–9.
   a. The rise of Solomon. Ch.1.
   b. The building and dedication of the temple. Chs. 2–7.
      (May be broken at ch. 5.)
   c. The greatness of Solomon. Chs. 8, 9.
2. The early days of Judah. Chs. 10–16.
   a. The weakness of the first two reigns. Chs. 10–13.
   b. The recovery under Asa. Chs. 14–16.
   c. The policies and piety of Jehoshaphat. Chs. 17–20.
3. Revolution and the days of King Josiah. Chs. 21–24.
4. Prosperity and disintegration. Chs. 25–28.
5. Hezekiah and the strength of faith. Chs. 29–32.
      (May be broken at ch. 31.)
6. Reaction, and Josiah's noble attempt at reform. 33: 1–35: 19.
7. The swift decline of Judah. 35: 20–36: 23.

Harmony of Samuel, Kings, and Chronicles

For the benefit of those who wish to make one reading of the
days of the Israelitish kingdom, the following harmony of parallel

passages in II Samuel, I & II Kings, with I & II Chronicles is outlined. In each column reference is made to the units of reading listed
above under each of these books separately, and the reference to the
passages from the books is also given. Thus, under II Samuel, "1, a"
refers to shorter unit "a" under larger unit "1," as listed above under
II Samuel. Sometimes the parallelism applies to only part of a unit.

The parallelism suggested below is sometimes that of similar
thought content, sometimes only that of approximately the same
period of time. Contrasts as well as comparisons will appear.

I Samuel	*I Chronicles*
3,e. 28: 3–31: 13.	2,a. Ch. 10.
II Samuel	
1. Chs. 1–4.	No parallel.
2. Chs. 5–7.	2,b. Chs. 13–17.
3. Chs. 8–10.	2,a. Chs. 11, 12;
	2,c. Chs. 18–20;
	2,d. Chs. 22–28.
4. Chs. 11, 12;	
5. Chs. 13, 14;	2,c. Ch. 21.
6. Chs. 15–20.	
7. Chs. 21–24.	2,d. Ch. 29.
I Kings	*II Chronicles*
1,a,b. Chs. 1–4.	1,a. Ch. 1.
1,c. 5: 1–9: 9.	1,b. Chs. 2–7.
(Break at ch. 8)	(Break at ch. 5)
1,d. 9: 10–11: 43.	1,c. Chs. 8, 9.
2,a. 12: 1–14: 20.	2,a. Chs. 10–13.
2,b. 14: 21–16: 20.	2,b. Chs. 14–16.
3,a. 16: 21–19: 21.	
b. Chs. 20, 21.	No parallel.
c. Ch. 22.	
II Kings	
1,a. Chs. 1–3.	No parallel.
No parallel.	2,c. Chs. 17–20.

1,b. Chs. 4–8.	No parallel.
(Broken at ch. 5 or 6)	
2. Chs. 9–11.	3. Chs. 21–24.
3,a,b. Chs. 12–16.	4. Chs. 25–28.
3,b. Ch. 17.	No parallel.
4. Chs. 18–20. (Isa., chs. 36–39)	5. Chs. 29–32.

(This history of Hezekiah is written in three books.)

5. 21: 1–23: 30.	6. 33: 1–35: 19.
6. 23: 31–25: 30.	7. 35: 20–36: 23.

Ezra—Nehemiah

That the books of Ezra and Nehemiah are closely related is easy to see. But just what the relation is in detail is not so clear. Both deal with the period of the attempt to rebuild the fortunes of the Jewish state after the return from the exile in Babylon. This period stretched over a century and a half. Whether the reformers Ezra and Nehemiah were contemporaries or whether they ever met in Jerusalem are questions in dispute. The average reader will perhaps be content to note that each rendered distinguished service in an effort to purify and reconstruct the remnant of the Jews seeking to realize their new freedom.

In this work of the renewal of the nation Ezra and Nehemiah were faced with the understandable temptation to become narrow. If the people were not to repeat their follies of pre-exilic days and succumb to the culture of surrounding pagans, they must be held to their faith by strictest ties. So it was that not only a literal wall was built around the city, but the people were walled in from communication with the life around them. Intermarriage was strictly forbidden, national customs were stressed to the point of legalism, and the law was meticulously enforced. Ezra is often referred to as "the father of Judaism"—the Judaism that went far beyond the law of Moses and brought on Jesus' condemnation of hypocrisy and led to Paul's rebellion.

Ezra: Units of Service Rendered

1. Ezra's work in rebuilding the temple. Chs. 1–6.
   (Skip through ch. 2, the list of those returning with Ezra to Jerusalem. The reading may be broken, if necessary, at ch. 5, though it is a distinct unit.)
2. Ezra's work of purifying families. Chs. 7–10.
   (Skip the lists in the first half of ch. 8 and the latter part of ch. 10.)

Nehemiah: Units of Service Rendered

1. Nehemiah's preparation for his work. Chs. 1, 2.
2. Rebuilding the city walls. Chs. 3–7.
   (Skip the lists which comprise a large part of ch. 3 and most of ch. 7.)
3. The people's pledge of holiness. Chs. 8–10.
   (Omit the lists in the first part of ch. 10.)
4. Nehemiah's concluding services. Chs. 11–13.
   (Skipping through the lists again.)

Esther: Units of Dramatic Interest

The book of Esther is the story of dark days during the exile when a plot was abroad to massacre the Jews. It is the tale of plot and counterplot, for it glorifies the characters of Esther and her guardian, Mordecai, because they were able to effect better intrigues than their enemies. While the name of God nowhere occurs, the book is religious in tone, and in part the purpose of its writing seems to have been to explain the origin of the "Feast of Purim," the Jewish annual celebration of Esther's deliverance of her people. The note of Jewish nationalism is strong throughout.

As has been explained in chapter 3, the book is most effectively read as one unit. If, however, division is desired, the following two plans are suggested, depending on the reader's taste as to the points at which the interest of this intensely dramatic story reaches its most real climaxes.

The following units suggest one climax:

1. Plots and counterplots. Chs. 1–5.
2. The triumph of Esther and Mordecai. Chs. 6–10.

These units suggest other points of breathtaking interest:

1. Esther's "coming to the kingdom." Chs. 1, 2.
2. Plots and counterplots. Chs. 3–7.
3. The triumph of the Jews because of Esther. Chs. 8–10.

Job: Units of Dramatic Action

This is an intensely interesting study of problems that appeal to the experience of all mankind. It is a brave attempt to meet the religious philosophy of the day which complacently taught that outward prosperity proved inward righteousness and outward misery proved hidden sin.

It is important to note that the prologue to the book, consisting of chapters 1 and 2, and the epilogue, consisting of 42: 7–16, are in prose, while all the rest is in poetry. The importance of this lies in the fact that the common notion of the book of Job dealing with the question, "Why do the righteous suffer?" is only partly true. This is the question of the long dramatic debate between Job and his friends and the more youthful Elihu—debates which occupy all the poetic part of the book. That this question is never answered has left many a reader disappointed with the book of Job. But part of the purpose of the book is to show that this question is unanswerable to men because they cannot see as God sees. It is a question which can be debated only on the plane of limited human knowledge. The brief prose sections take us back of the scenes to the real question before the court of heaven, a question propounded sneeringly by Satan, "Will a man serve God for nought?" And this question is answered, to Satan's confusion and God's glory. Job does serve God, and that without knowing he will receive any reward. He does cling to his righteousness in spite of his repeated experiences of suffering and sorrow, yet he is so proud of his achievement that he does need the humbling that comes with the divine revelation.

1. Prologue in prose: the problem of righteousness. Chs. 1, 2.
2. First cycle of debate: the problem of suffering. Chs. 3–14.
   (May be broken at the beginning of any new speech, i. e., at chs. 4, 6, 8, 9, 11, 12.)
3. Second cycle of debate: the problem of sin and suffering. Chs. 15–21.
   (New speeches start at chs. 18, 19, 20, 21.)
4. Third cycle of debate: the problem of presumptuousness. Chs. 22–31.
   (New speeches start at chs. 23, 25, 27, 28, 29.)
5. Elihu, the young man of cunning. Chs. 32–37.
   (New speeches start at chs. 34, 35, 36.)
6. The Lord humbles Job. 38: 1–42: 6.
   (Should not be broken because of grandeur.)
7. Epilogue in prose: the reward of Job. 42: 7–16.

The Psalms: Units of Religious Feeling

It has already been pointed out in chapter 5 that the Psalter is the rich heritage of Christian as well as of Jewish devotion. It plays on every phase of human emotion. Inevitably, some of these emotions will be worthier than others, but all have their counterpart in modern experience. That such a variety of feeling can be made the subject of religious song is the highest testimony to the power of God to hold sway over human emotions.

The Book of Psalms may be read in many ways. Taking it straight through, one or more Psalms at a time, will give rewarding variety, though for the Christian it will often intermingle some of the finest with some of the less useful of the Psalms. Attractiveness to the reader will be gained by interspersing two or three of the Psalms every now and then with the reading of other parts of the Bible, so as to keep fresh the spirit of lyric devotion.

The Psalter as we have it is a collection of five books. Each of these five is in turn a collection of Psalms made at some point or other in Hebrew history, and has a sort of unity of its own. Just when the collection of the five books was made we do not know.

Their divisions are marked for the English reader in the Revised Standard Version of the Bible, and are as follows:

Book I. Psalms 1–41. A collection of lyrics of personal experience, with an introduction to the entire collection (Psalm 1).

Book II. Psalms 42–72. These are mostly songs of the goodness and greatness of God.

Book III. Psalms 73–89. Here is a short liturgical collection.

Book IV. Psalms 90–106. This group contains many of the anthems.

Book V. Psalms 107–150. Historical Psalms, Pilgrim Hymns, and Hallelujah choruses make up the most of this collection.

Briefer collections within these books, such as 46–48, 95–100, 111–118, 120–134, 146–150, have already been commented on in chapter 5. There too the thesis was proposed that the Psalms might well be read singly in accordance with their dominant emotion. Some sixteen of these emotions were illustrated, and it remains now to list the Psalms that may be said to belong under each of these heads. Obviously such a grouping cannot be dogmatically upheld. Many Psalms breathe many emotions. Some readers will perhaps feel in a few Psalms the dominance of some emotion other than the one suggested here. This is a list for convenience only. Occasionally a Psalm has been listed twice, in a few instances because its emotions seem so balanced as to suggest that none is dominant, more often to give it a setting as an individual Psalm and also as part of some special group to which it obviously belongs.

1. *Psalms of Adoration:* 24, 29, 47, 50, 66, 67, 68, 75, 76, 82, 93, 99, 100, 104, 111, 113, 115, 134, 135, 139, 145, 146, 147, 148, 149, 150. (Compare 115 and 135.)

2. *Psalms of Meditation:* 1, 8, 14, 15, 19, 32, 34, 36, 37, 49, 52, 53, 73, 84, 101, 112, 119, 127, 128, 133. (Compare 14 and 53.)

3. *Psalms of Trust:* 3, 4, 5, 7, 11, 16, 23, 31, 42–43, 46, 48, 54, 55, 56, 57, 62, 63, 64, 71, 91, 94, 102, 121, 125, 130, 131.

4. *Psalms of Complaint:* 13, 22, 35, 55, 69, 74, 77, 79, 88, 89, 120, 123, 129, 142.

5. *Psalms of Earnest Petition:* 5, 6, 9–10, 12, 17, 25, 28, 31, 38, 39, 41, 51, 61, 70, 79, 80, 90, 140, 141, 143.

6. *Penitential Psalms:* 25, 32, 38, 51, 130.

7. *Psalms of Thanksgiving and Gratitude:* 18, 27, 30, 32, 48, 50, 52,
    85, 92, 103, 107, 116, 117, 118, 124, 126, 136, 138, 144.
8. *Festal Psalms:* 24, 33, 95–100, 118, 120–134.
9. *Liturgies:* 25, 26, 40, 65, 86.
10. *Historical Psalms:* 44, 68, 78, 81, 89, 105, 106, 114, 132.
11. *War Psalms:* 20, 21, 59, 60, 76, 108, 144.
12. *Messianic Psalms:* 2, 22, 45, 72, 110.
13. *Imprecatory Psalms:* 35, 58, 59, 69, 83, 109, 129, 137, 140.
14. *Psalms of the Glorification of Zion:* 84, 87, 122, 137.
15. *Psalms of the Law:* 1, 19, 119.
16. *Psalms of the Future Life:* 16, 17, 49, 73.

Of these classifications Nos. 1–7 contain Psalms which on the whole will have a more universal appeal than those in the remaining classes. Nos. 8–16 are more distinctly Jewish in their point of view. Every now and then, however, these groups contain some Psalm that has been spiritualized in Christian thought until its beauty has become full of meaning to us.

THE PROVERBS: UNITS OF PRACTICAL WISDOM

The habit of expressing truth in the form of short, pungent sayings is older than history and is common to all peoples. Every race has its proverbs. Small wonder then that the Hebrews, among whom the wisdom that is from above so early came to rule the thoughts about everyday living, should have developed the proverb form in such rich variety.

The proverbs of the Bible can hardly be called philosophy in the sense that the Greeks thought of philosophy, that is, as an orderly and logical arrangement of thought, a formal system. But they do represent serious thinking about life. They express seasoned understanding of the business of living, especially of the canny, sagacious kind that knows how to drive a good bargain or get the most out of a situation. This is not said in disparagement of the proverbs of the Bible. Often they are deep, and sometimes quite spiritual. But for the most part they are "practical," in the best sense of that word. They abound in the kind of wisdom that thoughtful experience produces. They treat of morals in many phases, and of prudence above all. They especially abound in counsel for young men to obey their parents, to avoid profligate living, and to use time and wealth well.

Not all the proverbs of the Bible are to be found in the book bearing that name. We see them in the riddles of Samson in the book of Judges. We run into many of them intermingled with the observations of the "preacher" of Ecclesiastes. The sayings of Jesus and of other writers of our New Testament abound in them.

This particular book boasts two kinds of proverbs, the "unit proverb," which is complete in one couplet that forms a single verse in our Bible, and the "proverb cluster," which is often a development at some length of some wisdom theme. The apostrophe to "Wisdom" (ch. 8, especially verses 22–31) is, in both thought and language, a forerunner of the prologue to John's Gospel. Like the book of Psalms, the book of Proverbs contains five collections. The points where these are marked are the natural divisions for reading.

1. A collection of songs in praise of wisdom. Chs. 1–9.
   a. The wise son and the foolish. Chs. 1–4.
      (May be broken, if necessary, at ch. 3.)
   b. The wisdom of purity. Chs. 5–7.
   c. Wisdom personified. Chs. 8, 9.
2. A collection of proverb gems. 10: 1–22: 16.
      (These are all unit proverbs. The reader may stop anywhere. For once he can read by verses!)
3. A collection of "the words of the wise." 22: 17–24: 34.
4. Another collection of proverb gems. Chs. 25–29.
      (Again the reading may be broken at the end of any proverb, though here there are some longer than one verse.)
5. A collection of curious proverbs. Chs. 30, 31.
   a. The number proverbs of Agur. Ch. 30.
   b. The proverbs of Lemuel's mother. Ch. 31.

ECCLESIASTES: UNITS OF PRACTICAL WISDOM

The similarity of this book to the one preceding is easily recognized. Its proverbial character is pronounced. Yet this time the proverbs have to do mainly with the results of a certain planned experience to which the author set himself. The name of the book is so rendered in our English Bible as to describe this author as a "preacher." Perhaps this is the best we can do to represent the hortatory nature of the contents.

The book of Ecclesiastes is not, as so often supposed, blank pessimism. The "preacher" does indeed have to report that his experiment has proved the futility of trying to find satisfaction in pleasure, riches, fame, and all the others of his list. But he has a positive conclusion to gain from the total picture. It is the concluding exhortation: "Fear God, and keep his commandments; for this is the whole duty of man" (12: 13).

We have already noted that this is among the books that may well be read at one sitting; in this way the "preacher's" experiment will be most convincing. But shorter units may also be found.

a. The fruitless search. 1: 1–4: 16.
b. Proverbs of observation. 4: 17–7: 29.
c. Wisdom and folly in public affairs. Chs. 8–10.
d. The meaning of life. Chs. 11, 12.

THE SONG OF SOLOMON

This is, to the English reader, the strangest book in the Old Testament. It is a love song, or a series of love songs, abounding in imagery which, while never sensual, is often quite sensuous. It has shocked many good people to find a song of human loves in the Bible, and as a result they have allegorized it to mean the love of Christ for his church. But to the Hebrew, who believed profoundly that God was interested in all the affairs of life, it was not too much to expect a hymn of human affection in the sacred canon. The Christian will do well to rejoice in that exaltation of love.

Even so, the interpretation of this little book has puzzled many. To some it represents King Solomon, to whom the poem has long been attributed, wooing the daughter of Pharaoh. The many changes of speaker in the verses represent the conversation of this one lover with his one beloved, with side lines for choruses. To others, the poem is a hidden presentation of a conflict in the heart of a rustic maiden who is beloved by a youth of her own station but is wooed also by the king for her beauty. The constancy of her love finally wins out in the retirement of Solomon from the scene.

These varieties of interpretation are noted for the purpose of emphasizing that the reader will probably do well not to try to interpret too closely, but rather to revel in the lyric spirit of the lines and to glorify love with the author. For this reason the poem should be considered one unit. If reading must be broken, the best stopping places are at 4: 1; 5: 2; 7: 1; and 8: 5.

The Prophets

When the reader of the Bible comes to the prophets he finds more of the "preached Word" to which he is accustomed from the pulpit than in any other part of the Old Testament. The idea of a message to proclaim is central to all the prophets.

The vision messages and oracles of the prophets came to them direct from God. The religious principles proclaimed in these oracles are timeless. The prophets are our eternal contemporaries, with their insistence on the reality of sin, the need of repentance, the forgiving love of God, the willfulness of men, the prevalence of social evil, the need of redemption not only for the individual but also for the group. They are more distinctly the forerunners of Jesus and his gospel than any other of his predecessors.

Yet the messages of the prophets were always directly related to their own time. The prophets understood their day and spoke specifically to it. For this reason their messages are often best understood by reading the background of their time. And where can one better get this than in the biblical books of the history of the times to which the prophets spoke? For this reason it is often very worth while to read the prophets in conjunction with the appropriate portions of the historical books of the Old Testament. While there are a few cases in which we do not know the time, most of the prophets are dated. The following table suggests their interweaving with other books.

With II Kings, units 3 and 4, and with II Chronicles, units 4 and 5, as outlined above in the "Harmony of Samuel, Kings, and Chronicles," may be read those four illustrious prophets who spoke to the great age that Kings and Chronicles describe. They are Amos, Hosea, Micah, and Isaiah, chapters 1–39, and it will be well to read them in that order.

With II Kings, units 5 and 6, and with II Chronicles, units 6 and 7, may be read the prophecies of Jeremiah, Habakkuk, Zephaniah, Nahum, who spoke for the most part in the period of the decline of Judah.

In the days of the exile, it will be well to read against the background of such a book as Esther, or of the early chapters of description in Nehemiah, the prophecy of Ezekiel that deals entirely with the exile. The second half of the prophecy of Isaiah, chapters 40–66, may be most appropriately read here, for these lovely oracles bear the message of hope for deliverance from the bitterness of the exile.

The return to Palestine brings us face to face with Haggai and Zechariah, prophets of the rebuilding of the temple. They should be taken up along with the historical books of Ezra and Nehemiah. Malachi, the last of the prophets, goes well with the book of Ezra itself, for it has the same purpose of purifying the returned people, especially from mixed marriages.

It is difficult to date Joel and Obadiah and Jonah with any certainty, but they probably were written later than the others.

ISAIAH: THE SEER

Reading the prophets singly by their units of thought may appear to be a real task when one looks at the length of Isaiah that stands at their head. Yet this book is rich in imagery, varied in mood, full of lofty idealism, and often very close to the spirit of the Christian

message. The first thirty-nine chapters form a major unit in themselves. Most of the material here comes directly from the preaching
of Isaiah the son of Amoz who had ready access to court from the
balmy days of Uzziah king of Judah through the reigns of Ahaz
and Hezekiah. The prophet discusses religion in all its phases
against the background of a minute acquaintance with the politics
of the time. We shall do well to go back to II Kings, chapters 14–20,
to get our bearings. Isaiah speaks home to the heart of Judah, up-
braiding her for not knowing the Lord, for living in profligate ease
and thoughtless cruelty, for being the vine which the Lord had
planted and tended so carefully and yet being fruitless. He opens
his own heart and shows us the personal experience of his call (ch.
6). He denounces the politics of the day—going to Egypt for help,
making military alliances with Israel and Syria, paying tribute to
Assyria, and many other evil customs. He finds the weak King
Ahaz unresponsive to the whiplash of his denunciation, but Ahaz'
finer son, Hezekiah, trusts and follows the prophet.

In the units of reading suggested below, the whole of larger unit
1 contains doctrines that are found again in shorter unit 3,b.
Shorter unit 1,b has as its historical sequence 3,d. Parts of these
first thirty-nine chapters of the book of Isaiah are probably of later
date than the times to which we have referred, especially the sermon
on Babylon, 13: 1–14: 27 and the apocalypse of judgment, chapters
24–27. They may well have been added to Isaiah's book because
they breathe his spirit.

1. Messages to the people of Judah. Chs. 1–12.
    a. The description of their sin. Chs. 1–5.
       (May be broken for reading at ch. 3.)
    b. The challenge to faith, with especial reference to the cowardice of
       Ahaz. Chs. 6–12.
       (May be broken at 9: 8.)
2. Messages to or concerning other nations. Chs. 13–23.
    a. Babylon. 13: 1–14: 27.
    b. Small kingdoms bordering Palestine. 14: 28–17: 14.
    c. Kingdoms to the south. Chs. 18–21.

The tone and purpose of Isaiah, chapters 40–66, are in many ways quite different from those of the preceding chapters. While the same prophetic ardor, the same zeal for the holiness of God, and the same high idealism are to be found, the eye of the seer now looks, not at court conditions during the reigns of Judah's kings, but at the need of encouraging the exiles in their return from Babylon, two centuries after these kings of Judah had passed from the scene. Whether this same Isaiah was inspired to see beyond the days of Judah's shipwreck and weary pilgrimage from her land to the days of return from her captivity, or whether a later prophet in the spirit and faith of Isaiah spoke to the people of his day and his message was appended to that of Isaiah, in any case the situation in these chapters is the end of the exile and their vision is of deliverance and hope. In any case also the entire contents of the book of Isaiah belong in the one volume, for the theology of the holiness of God is the foundation of its structure. But in the major portion of the first thirty-nine chapters God's judgment upon sin is prominent, while in chapters 40–66 the redeeming grace of God and the work of his servant alternate as the chief themes.

In chapter 4 we have already suggested the division of chapters 40–66 into three larger reading units:

Perhaps an easier arrangement for the reader to follow is the following, also in three larger units, with closely related shorter units. Here the main dividing marks are the repeated utterance, "There is no peace for the wicked."

4. The redemptive love of God. Chs. 40–48.
   a. The God of the whole earth is redeemer. 40: 1–41: 7.
   b. The preparation of Israel as God's servant in redemption and of Cyrus to help her. 41: 8–45: 24.
      (May be broken at ch. 43, and at 44: 24.)
   c. The downfall of Babylon, her gods and her glory, with the deliverance of Israel from this historic enemy. Chs. 46–48.
5. The ministry of the Servant in redemption. Chs. 49–57.
   a. To restore Israel. 49: 1–52: 12.
      (May be broken at ch. 51.)
   b. To suffer vicariously. 52: 13–53: 12.
   c. To bring both encouragement and warning to the people. Chs. 54–57.
      (May be broken, if necessary, at ch. 56.)
6. The redeemed people. Chs. 58–66.
   a. True and false worship. Ch. 58.
   b. Sin confessed and the people redeemed. Ch. 59.
   c. The glory of the redeemed city. Ch. 60.
   d. The preaching of redemption. Chs. 61, 62.
   e. An impassioned prayer to the God of redemption. Chs. 63, 64.
   f. Blessings on the faithful and doom on the unfaithful. Chs. 65, 66.

JEREMIAH: PROPHET OF THE NEW COVENANT

It is difficult to read the book of Jeremiah. For one thing there is often little order to the thought. This may be due in part to the fact that Jeremiah's first writing down of his prophecies was burned by a hostile king (36: 21–23). For another thing, prophetic utterances and historical notes are often interwoven in a way that is difficult for one to follow who is not familiar with the details of the history of the times. And most important is it to note that in Jeremiah himself we have the classic example of a prophet whose feelings often run away with him, who has showed us his heart as unashamedly in his writings as he showed it to Judah in his speech, and who frequently breaks off in the midst of preaching to his people that he may bemoan his personal lot. We know a great deal about the man and his experiences from reading his book. But he interweaves little dirges of feeling so often with his messages that he is hard to follow. Moreover, if the longer units of reading are to be broken at all into shorter units, these latter must often be quite short to make any sense at all standing by themselves. We shall note these short units, but suggest by means of the bracketing of several of them together that two or more of these shorter units may often be read at once so that disproportionate time may not be spent on the details of Jeremiah's agony.

But the reader must not get the impression that Jeremiah's lack of chronological order or the recurrent theme of the prophet's personal troubles leaves the message wanting. Here is an impassioned theology of the Lord's pleading with his people, of the utter falsity of dependence on ritual, of the meaning and need of true repentance, and especially of that new covenant which God shall write, not again on tables of stone, but on the tablets of men's hearts. Here is the emphasis on the responsibility of the individual at the time when the nation is going to pieces. And here also is one of the greatest patriots that ever lived, a lover of his nation who was misunderstood and counted as an enemy by the very ones he loved the most. No wonder men thought Jesus was a new Jeremiah (Matt. 16: 14).

1. The prophet's call and basic message. Chs. 1–6.
   a. The call. Ch. 1.
   b. The sin of Judah. 2: 1–4: 4.
   c. Judgment coming at the hands of a foreign foe. 4: 5–6: 30.
      (Broken, if necessary, at 5: 20.)
2. The analysis of Judah's sin. Chs. 7–10.
   a. The prophet's address on sin, delivered in the court of the temple. 7: 1–8: 17.
   b. An ecstasy of grief. 8: 18–9: 26.
   c. Idolatry and doom. Ch. 10.

3. The preaching of judgment. Chs. 11–17.
    a. The broken covenant. 11: 1–17.
    b. The plot against the prophet and his appeal to God. 11: 18–12: 6.
    c. Judgment on Judah and her neighbors. 12: 7–17.
    d. Emblematic preaching of judgment. Ch. 13.
    e. The drought as judgment. 14: 1–15: 9.
    f. The loneliness of the prophet of judgment. 15: 10–16: 21.
    g. Sin, doom, and hope. Ch. 17.
4. Parables of pottery, interwoven with personal experiences of the prophet. Chs. 18–20.
    (Should be read as one for real effect.)
    a. The potter. 18: 1–17.
    b. A plot against Jeremiah. 18: 18–23.
    c. The broken bottle. Ch. 19.
    d. In the stocks. Ch. 20.
5. Prophecies delivered to rulers. Chs. 21–23.
    a. Prophecies concerning four of Judah's kings and a true king to come. 21: 1–23: 8.
    b. Warning against the effect of false prophets on the realm. 23: 9–40.
6. Prophecies related to the exile of Judah. Chs. 24–29.
    a. The parable of the figs. Ch. 24.
    b. The Lord's impending fury. Ch. 25.
    c. Prophecy of the destruction of the temple. Ch. 26.
    d. The yoke of Babylon. Chs. 27, 28.
    e. A letter to the exiles. Ch. 29.
7. Prophecies of restoration. Chs. 30, 31.
    (These are too fine to be broken. Note, especially, the New Covenant, 31: 31–34.)
8. Prophecies growing out of historical incidents. Chs. 32–45.
    a. Jeremiah's family inheritance. Ch. 32.
    b. Future blessings. Ch. 33.
    c. A warning to Zedekiah, resulting from a broken promise. Ch. 34.
    d. The good example of the Rechabites. Ch. 35.
    e. The burning of the scroll. Ch. 36.
    f. Jeremiah and King Zedekiah at the fall of Jerusalem. 37: 1–39: 12.
    g. Jeremiah in Jerusalem after its capture. 39: 12–41: 18.
    h. Jeremiah in Egypt. Chs. 42–45.
    (Broken, if necessary, at ch. 44.)

9. Prophecies against foreign nations. Chs. 46–51.
   a. Against Egypt. Ch. 46.
   b. Against the Philistines. Ch. 47.
   c. Against Moab. Ch. 48.
   d. Against Ammonites, Edomites, Syrians, and others. Ch. 49.
   e. Against Babylon. Chs. 50, 51.
      (May be broken at ch. 51.)
10. Historical appendage to the book: the story of the fall of Jerusalem. Ch. 52.

THE LAMENTATIONS OF JEREMIAH

This formal dirge, acrostic in arrangement, has been attributed traditionally to Jeremiah, and associated with his prophecy at the time of the fall of Jerusalem, though it is more generally considered to be of later date. It may well be read at one sitting. But four of the five chapters are acrostic; that is, the first verse of each begins in Hebrew with the first of the twenty-two letters of the Hebrew alphabet, the second with the second letter, and so on, save that in the third chapter the first three verses begin with the first letter, the next three with the second, so that there are sixty-six verses in this chapter to twenty-two in the others. Hence, reading may be broken at the beginning of any chapter, or the first two chapters may be taken together, the third separately, and the other two together.

As a matter of fact the theme of lament differs a little in each chapter. This is excellently brought out in the titles given the chapters in the Smith and Goodspeed Bible:

Ch. 1. "The desolation and misery of conquered Jerusalem."
Ch. 2. "God's judgment on Jerusalem."
Ch. 3. "Jerusalem's lament and prayer."
Ch. 4. "The contrast between Jerusalem's past and present."
Ch. 5. "The nation's prayer for compassion."

EZEKIEL: PROPHET OF THE MAJESTY OF GOD

The prophecy of Ezekiel is broken in two by what was to him the climactic event of his day, the final capture of the holy city.

The capture is not announced until 33: 21. Up to this point the prophet, who is most of the time in Babylon with those who were exiled earlier, ministers to them and seeks, with many symbols and acted parables, to warn the people back home so that the city may escape calamity. He describes for them his famous vision of the moving chariot of God (ch. 1). He pinpoints all of Judah's sin on the basic evil of idolatry (ch. 8). He mingles in his strange and awful figures the woes of the sinful people and his own depression, a depression brought to personal climax in the death of the prophet's wife (ch. 24).

But all to no avail. Judah continues on her willful way and falls to the captor. Then it is that the prophet, still the man of God even in defeat, turns first to oracles against foreign nations (chs. 25–32) and then, for the remainder of his book, to the encouragement and upbuilding of the exiles. He develops Jeremiah's doctrine that the individual is the responsible person now that the nation has fallen (ch. 33). He bids the exiles settle down, raise families, and be content with their lot. On the other hand he insists that they shall not intermingle with the paganism about them but that they shall continue to worship the Lord even without the temple. This reminds us of the Psalmist of the first part of Psalm 137 who found it so difficult to sing the Lord's song in a strange land.

But Ezekiel is also a prophet of hope. He preaches regeneration as the ground of the new order (ch. 37); he anticipates a true shepherd instead of the false shepherds that have eaten the flock (ch. 34). And, as the one great man of God in the Old Testament who actually served both as prophet and as priest, Ezekiel sees the restoration of God's people in terms of a new temple built according to exact prescriptions, and fitted for the unending worship of God (chs. 40–48).

In the following reading outline, some of the shorter units are again bracketed for reading together.

1. The prophet called and commissioned. Chs. 1–3.
2. The mimic seige of Jerusalem, with symbols of her fall. Chs. 4, 5.
3. The doom of the people of Israel. Chs. 6, 7.

4. A realistic vision of Jerusalem's hideous life. Chs. 8–11.
5. Approaching exile. Chs. 12–14.
6. A series of allegories. Chs. 15–19.
    a. The vine. Ch. 15.
    b. The faithless wife. Ch. 16.
    c. The eagle and the vine. Ch. 17.
       (Units a and c may well be read together.)
    d. Sour grapes. Ch. 18.
    e. Lions and vineyards. Ch. 19.
7. The approaching end. Chs. 20–24.
    a. The inquiring elders. 20: 1–44.
    b. Judgment by fire and sword. 20: 45–21: 32.
    c. The city of blood and dross. Ch. 22.
    d. The two sisters. Ch. 23.
    e. The kettle of judgment. 24: 1–14.
    f. The prophet's personal woe. 24: 15–27.
8. Prophecies against the nations. Chs. 25–32.
    a. Various neighbors. Ch. 25.
    b. Tyre and Sidon. Chs. 26–28.
    c. Egypt. Chs. 29–32.
       (May be broken at ch. 31.)
9. The fall of Jerusalem. Chs. 33–35.
    a. The prophet as watchman. 33: 1–20.
    b. The capture of Jerusalem. 33: 21–33.
    c. False shepherds. Ch. 34.
    d. The enemy on Mt. Seir. Ch. 35.
10. The restoration of Israel. Chs. 36–48.
    a. God's good purpose. 36: 1–15.
    b. The preaching of regeneration. 36: 16–37: 14.
    c. New unity. 37: 15–28.
    d. The overthrow of enemies, personified as "Gog," and "Magog." Chs. 38, 39.
    e. The new temple. Chs. 40–42.
    f. The new worship. Chs. 43–46.
       (The details of these chapters may be skipped through, though comparisons to the description of the desert tabernacle in Exodus, chs. 25–31, may prove interesting to some.)
    g. The stream of life in a renewed land. Chs. 47, 48.

Daniel: Narrative and Vision

The book of Daniel falls neatly into two parts, each containing six chapters. The first six relate the personal experiences of Daniel, an exile in the days of the Babylonian captivity. They form an excellent story unit, though each chapter is a smaller story in itself. The latter six chapters contain apocalyptic visions, credited to Daniel. They are related to the first part, in that the dream of Nebuchadnezzar, described in chapter 2, presents the basic imagery of the visions of chapters 7–12. The apocalyptic nature of these visions will be discussed later in this book (ch. 11). It is, however, of very little use for the average Christian to read these last six chapters of Daniel without having at hand a sensible commentary to review for him the history of which they are so vivid, yet so enigmatic, an interpretation.

1. The personal experiences of Daniel during the exile. Chs. 1–6.
   a. The four courageous youths. Ch. 1.
   b. Nebuchadnezzar's dream. Ch. 2.
   c. In the fiery furnace. Ch. 3.
   d. Nebuchadnezzar goes insane. Ch. 4.
   e. Belshazzar's feast. Ch. 5.
   f. In the lions' den. Ch. 6.
2. The apocalyptic visions of Daniel. Chs. 7–12.
   a. The four beasts. Ch. 7.
   b. The ram and the he-goat. Ch. 8.
   c. The seventy weeks. Ch. 9.
   d. Kingdom against kingdom. Chs. 10–12.

The Minor Prophets

The remainder of the Old Testament is composed of the twelve "Minor Prophets," so called simply because they are shorter than the books of Isaiah, Jeremiah, Ezekiel, and Daniel. Each of them may well be read as a unit. Some of them can hardly be divided, though several have distinctive breaks in their thought.

HOSEA: PROPHET OF GOD'S LOVE

The message of Hosea was delivered to northern Israel in the days of the illustrious Jeroboam II. It is a wonderful medley of the realism of sin, a heartfelt call to repentance, and the picturing of the knowledge and the love of God. Deep is its impression of the grace of God overcoming even unthinking sin. The prophet's terrible experience in his own broken home furnishes the key to his marvelous understanding of the nature of Israel's broken tryst with God.

1. The story of the unfaithful wife. Chs. 1–3.
2. Israel's unfaithfulness in morality. 4: 1–7: 7.
3. Israel's unfaithfulness in political policy. 7: 8–10: 15.
4. The redemptive love of God. Chs. 11–14.

JOEL: A VIVID PICTURE OF DOOM

This picturesque prophecy describes, under the symbols of a severe locust plague, the coming of devastating judgment. Joel calls this judgment "the day of the Lord." The prophecy should be read as a unit. The first two chapters contain the vivid imagery, while the proclamation of judgment is reserved for the third chapter. The book ends peacefully with a beautiful vision of the days of reclamation beyond judgment.

AMOS: PROPHET OF GOD'S RIGHTEOUSNESS

Like Hosea, the words of Amos were addressed to northern Israel in the days of Jeroboam II. But unlike Hosea, the book of Amos has little to say about the grace or love of God. Amos is the stern man from the hills, rugged and rustic. His message abounds in rural imagery and in the thundering tones of justice. He has seen cruel injustice of all kinds, especially in such cities as Samaria, Bethel, and Gilgal. His denunciation is as unsparing as his insight is keen.

1. The same God judges all nations according to their light. Chs. 1, 2.
2. Judgment on Israel's immoral civilization and her merely formal religion. Chs. 3–6.
   (A fine unit to impress the moral imperative of life, but it may be broken, if absolutely necessary, at ch. 5.)
3. Amos's visions of judgment and restoration. Chs. 7–9.

OBADIAH: REVENGE ON EDOM

This little leaf from a prophet's notebook is a unit of fearful judgment on Israel's neighboring enemy, Edom. Its date is uncertain, for there were several occasions in the history of God's people when the Edomites egged others on to Israel's destruction, as they are here pictured doing.

JONAH: UNWILLING PROPHET OF GOD'S FORGIVING LOVE

Everyone knows something of the story of Jonah's experiences. But many remember the unessential and forget the all-important. We have already showed (ch. 3) that the four chapters of this little book must be read as one to get the proper impression, that of showing the sin and selfishness of narrow nationalism and the necessity for understanding the yearning love of God. That this love extends to a powerful and wicked enemy may be as hard to learn in the midst of modern international hatreds as it was for Jonah in the days of Nineveh's dictatorship over Israel's world. The missionary spirit has ever come hard when it extends to enemy aliens.

MICAH: PROPHET WITH CONCERN FOR THE POOR

It was probably to be expected that in the prophetic line which was to culminate in him who had "nowhere to lay his head" there should be one prophet who concerned himself with poor people just because they were poor. Micah was a younger contemporary of Hosea and Amos. He spoke mostly, however, to southern Judah.

He spoke of the rural districts while the great Isaiah was laboring in the capital (ch. 1). There is much in common between the two, as has been illustrated by their nearly identical messages on peace (Micah 4: 1–5; Isa. 2: 1–4).

But Micah is especially noteworthy for his classification of kinds of sins according to the kinds of people—the sins of kings, nobles, priests, false prophets, and the like (chs. 2, 3). He is almost unique in beginning with the present situation, going to a glorious vision of the future, and then returning to the present. He is remembered most frequently for his great description of God's requirement (6: 8). A sense of the richness of religion awaits the reader who takes Micah at a sitting, but the following units are not amiss.

1. The march of judgment through the land. Ch. 1.
2. The case of the poor against the rich. Chs. 2, 3.
3. The future hope. Chs. 4, 5.
4. The inglorious present with its needs. Chs. 6, 7.

NAHUM: THE DOOM OF NINEVEH

We have showed in chapter 5 that this prophecy is a unit of feeling. It is to be compared with Joel in intense vividness. It is to be contrasted with Jonah, in that it proclaims the doom of Nineveh at a time when the cup of her iniquity was full, as over against the book of Jonah's teaching of the love of God for Nineveh. The book should be read at one sitting to see how one outraged people may find in the doom of its oppressor the judgment of God. If absolutely necessary, the reading may be broken at chapter 3.

HABAKKUK: PROPHET OF DOUBT
TRANSFORMED BY FAITH

This is a very fine prophetic unit, portraying from the prophet's own experience the triumph of faith over doubt. Habakkuk, questioning God's justice in the face of the invasion of his land by the feared Chaldeans, comes to understand the providence contained in God's judgments and concludes with a prayer of thanksgiving for God himself. The book is noteworthy for its memorable quotes: 2: 4, 14, 20. The first of these is of especial significance, since it was the basis of Paul's doctrine of faith (Gal. 3: 11), and this in turn was Luther's clarion call to the Reformation. Habakkuk's prayer (ch. 3) may be read separately if necessary.

Zephaniah: Judgment and Redemption

Like Joel, the book of Zephaniah is a unit of prophecy describing "the day of the Lord." For the best results this too should be read at one sitting, but it breaks into the following two moods, treated at unequal length:

The day of the Lord is a day of doom. 1: 1–3: 7.
There is redemptive purpose in God's judgments. 3: 8–20.

Haggai: A Plain Man's Task Well Done

The last three prophets have to do with the days of restoration in Jerusalem following the exile.

The book of Haggai is the chronicle of a prosaic prophet who was given the task of stirring up an indifferent people to rebuild the fallen temple. This little collection of brief oracles, carefully dated, shows how well he succeeded in this particular work. These oracles have to do in turn with the call of the Lord to the people to consider how they fare in comparison with the condition of the temple, a promise of an outpouring of blessing, a question on holiness, and a special message to Zerubbabel their leader.

Zechariah: Visions of Renewal

Like Daniel, the book of Zechariah falls into two distinct parts. The first eight chapters are similar to Haggai in that they present the immediate human task of rebuilding Jerusalem. But they are set in vision imagery that reminds us again of Daniel.

The last six chapters of Zechariah are apocalyptic in form, revealing the glorious future God has in store for Jerusalem. They consist of two oracles of reassurance and comfort.

1. Visions associated with the rebuilding of Jerusalem. Chs. 1–8.
   a. Visions of encouragement to activity. Chs. 1, 2.
   b. Visions of Judah's two leaders, Joshua and Zerubbabel. Chs. 3, 4.
   c. Visions of judgment on Jerusalem's foes. 5: 1–6: 8.
   d. Promise of fulfillment to Jerusalem. 6: 9–8: 23.
2. The glorious future of Jerusalem. Chs. 9–14.
   a. An oracle of God's blessing on his redeemed people. Chs. 9–11.
   b. An oracle of God's shepherd and the day of the Lord. Chs. 12–14.

MALACHI: MY MESSENGER

The word "Malachi" means "My messenger." It may be a sort of title given to a prophet, rather than a name. The prophet of this brief message came late on the scene, after the reconstruction of Jerusalem had raised new problems of purity in worship and freedom from unwholesome alliances with surrounding tribes. He blends with these considerations the apocalyptic imagery and the Messianic hope, as well as the distinct expectancy of a forerunner of the coming of the Lord—an expectancy applied in the New Testament to John the Baptist.

If absolutely necessary this little book may be broken at 2: 17, but its message is most effective if read as a unit, harmonizing as it does many of the chief elements of Old Testament prophecy in this, its closing oracle.

Chapter 8

UNITS OF READING
IN THE NEW TESTAMENT

The New Testament is the Christian's charter of life. He will find fresh interest with each reading, especially if he varies his method. Here he can well afford to read by shorter units than in the case of the Old Testament, for the bearing of each part on his immediate life will be more evident. There is plenty of room for slow, careful reading with much meditation. Nevertheless, even in the New Testament, longer units are often desirable in order that the reader may get the sweep of the larger purpose. Hence we shall still encourage reading of the Bible in larger amounts at once. This will help give the thrill of seeing the woods in perspective, where before only individual trees have been examined.

THE GOSPELS

The earliest writings of our New Testament were probably some of the letters. It is likely that almost all of the epistles of Paul were written before any one of our Gospels was completed. Nevertheless the Gospels properly stand at the beginning of our New Testament, for they tell the story of that life which lies behind the writing of each of these twenty-seven documents.

Of the many different ways in which the Gospels may be read, the most obvious is to follow each by itself as a story of Jesus in its own right. And this needs doing often, for in spite of the many similarities and even exact repetitions in the Gospels, each one has its own point of view and its own distinct purpose.

In these outlines we shall emphasize the longer units in reading each Gospel by itself, reserving for a plan of reading the Gospels together the stress on shorter units from each.

MATTHEW: THE GOSPEL OF THE OLD TESTAMENT MESSIAH

It is appropriate that the Gospel of Matthew should stand at the head of the list. Not only does it contain some of the earliest written material recounting the teachings of Jesus, but it is also the New Testament's closest link with the Old. More quotations and references from Old Testament books are to be found in Matthew than in the other Gospels combined.

The reason for this lies in a paradox. The Gospel of Matthew is at once very Jewish in its outlook and very anti-Jewish in its sentiments. We do not of course know the exact connection of the apostle Matthew with our first Gospel. But traditionally he compiled an early account of the teachings of Jesus. Now Matthew himself had been grounded in the law. But he was also a tax-collector for Rome, and so a social low-caste among his own people. He must have been eyewitness with poignant understanding of the persecution of Jesus by the religious leaders of the Jews for eating with "sinners." Yet he saw in Jesus a potentate worthier than any from Rome, and the ideal of Jesus' kingdom gripped him. He was well equipped to appeal to his own people from their own scriptures to show them that Jesus' kingdom was the true fulfillment of the Messianic kingdom dreamed by prophets and psalmists.

The Gospel of Matthew drives home the new message of the kingdom by collecting Jesus' sayings about it into various sermons or discourses. We have long called the first of these the "Sermon on the Mount." Its theme is really the righteousness of the kingdom which must exceed that of the law. But scholars generally recognize as other sermons in Matthew the collection of missionary injunctions in chapter 10, the group of kingdom parables in chapter 13, the discourse on humility in chapter 18, and that on the eschatology of the kingdom in chapters 24 and 25.

1. The preparation of Jesus for his work. Chs. 1–4.
   a. The days of infancy. Chs. 1, 2.
   b. The public appearance and test. Chs. 3, 4.
2. The "Magna Charta" of Jesus' kingdom. Chs. 5–7.
3. Jesus, the miracle worker. Chs. 8, 9.
4. The mission and message of the kingdom. Chs. 10–13.
   a. The mission of the kingdom. Ch. 10.
   b. Kingdom activities taught and illustrated. Chs. 11, 12.
   c. Parables of the kingdom. Ch. 13.
5. Public ministry in Galilee in the face of Pharisaic opposition. 14: 1–16: 12.
6. Private ministry of Jesus to his disciples. 16: 13–18: 35.
   a. Stressing his own coming humiliation in death. 16: 13–17: 27.
   b. Stressing their need of humility. Ch. 18.
7. Jesus goes up to Jerusalem with his disciples. 19: 1–21: 22.
8. Controversies in the temple courts. 21: 23–23: 39.
9. Jesus' discourse on "last things." Chs. 24, 25.
10. From retirement to glory. Chs. 26–28.
    a. The fellowship of the upper room and the loneliness of the garden. 26: 1–56.
    b. The trial of Jesus. 26: 57–27: 31.
    c. The crucifixion and resurrection. 27: 32–28: 20.

Mark: The Gospel of the Servant

The Gospel of Mark is the shortest of the four. Fifteen-sixteenths of its contents are to be found in one or more of the other Gospels. Why then should it ever have been preserved? Because its point of view is unique. The same stories, when told in Mark, take on new vigor and assume the proportions of the spectacular, as we realize that Mark paints a glowing picture of Jesus as the most active of heroes, the most vivid of personalities, the most colorful of the masters of men. It is Mark's method, his choice of words, that enables him to present the gospel so realistically.

Plunging right into his narrative of Jesus' activity without any introduction on the days of the infancy, Mark displays Jesus going "immediately" here and "immediately" there. Except for the fourth and thirteenth chapters, there is little of the grouped teaching that occupies so much space in Matthew. Mark combines swift movement with a lingering over dramatic detail. He presents the pithy sayings of Jesus as pronouncements upon stupendous events. These occurrences are generally responses of large crowds to the preaching that "the kingdom of God is at hand," and they highlight Jesus' compassion on the forgotten and the needy.

Traditionally, Mark who was at first the companion of Barnabas and Paul later became associated with Peter and wrote down the gospel as he heard Peter preach it. Hence the vividness and the interest in Jesus' deeds.

If the reader omits from the Gospel of Matthew the sections on the infancy and such great teaching discourses as those we listed, he will find that the first and second Gospels follow much the same pattern of events, though not always in the same order. In the following reading units for Mark we have noted passages parallel to Matthew, so that these two Gospels may easily be read side by side:

1. The early ministry of Jesus. 1: 1–3: 6.
   (Cf. Matthew, unit 3.)
2. Jesus the Master. 3: 7–6: 13.
   a. Of his disciples and himself. 3: 7–35.
   b. Of parabolic teaching. 4: 1–34.
   c. Of disease and death. 4: 35–6: 13.
   (Cf. Matthew, parts of units 3, 4.)
3. Completion of the Galilean ministry in the face of opposition. 6: 14–8: 26.
   (Cf. Matthew, unit 5.)
4. The meaning of the cross. 8: 27–9: 50.
   (Cf. Matthew, unit 6.)
5. Going up to Jerusalem. 10: 1–11: 26.
   (Cf. Matthew, unit 7.)
6. Controversies in the temple courts. 11: 27–12: 44.
   (Cf. Matthew, unit 8.)
7. Jesus' discourse on "last things." Ch. 13.
   (Cf. Matthew, unit 9.)
8. From retirement to glory. Chs. 14–16.
   a. The upper room and the lonely garden. 14: 1–52.

b. The trial of Jesus. 14: 53–15: 20.
c. The crucifixion and resurrection. 15: 21–16: 8.
   (Cf. Matthew, unit 10.)

Luke: The Gospel of the Lover of Humanity

The Gospel of Luke follows an order of events in the life of Jesus quite similar to that in Mark. Added to this it has many of the teachings of Jesus that are stressed by Matthew; but instead of having them in collected form such as Matthew's "Sermon on the Mount," it has them scattered through the narrative of events, often connecting a short teaching with some circumstance out of which it grew. But Luke has some choice material all his own, for here are many parables that occur nowhere else. Most of them, as also most of the short teachings referred to above, occur in the great central section of the Gospel of Luke, between chapters 9 and 19, where this Gentile writer presents Jesus ministering for the most part outside the territory of the Jews. For this is the Gospel that illustrates more than any other the love of Jesus for men as men, a love that knew no bounds of race or class. "The Son of man came to seek and to save the lost" (19: 10) is the golden text of Luke. In this great central section there stand out such parables as the Good Samaritan, the Prodigal Son, the Friend at Midnight, the Widow without a Friend, the Rich Man and the Beggar, and many others that breathe social passion for the unfortunate. This same passion is the keynote of the song of Jesus' mother at his birth, and of others of the songs and prayers that distinguish this beautiful poetic Gospel.

All these characteristics of our third Gospel may be related to Luke's traditional vocation as a physician. He also was an early companion of Paul, and he may have learned from the great apostle the concern for salvation that is so marked in his pages. Luke stresses also the devotional life; there is much reference to prayer. And he loves to idealize people by putting all their actions in the best possible light. His fondness for women characters and especially for widows fits with these other traits.

Because of the brevity of much of the teaching material, it is easier to break the Gospel of Luke into satisfactory "shorter units" than either of the two that precede it. Of special note is the fact that Luke gives scanty treatment to the final controversies of Jesus in Jerusalem which are more extended in Mark and of great length in Matthew.

1. The infancy of Jesus. Chs. 1, 2.
    a. Annunciations of John and Jesus. 1: 1–56.
    b. Births of John and Jesus. 1: 57–2: 52.
       (Compare and contrast Matthew, unit 1,a.)
2. Jesus' preparation and early ministry. Chs. 3, 4.
       (Cf. Matthew, unit 1,b.)
3. The early Galilean ministry. 5: 1–6: 11.
       (Cf. Matthew, unit 3; Mark, unit 1.)
4. Ministering with the disciples. 6: 12–8: 56.
    a. A preaching tour. 6: 12–8: 3.
    b. Teaching and healing. 8: 4–56.
       (With 4,b, cf. Mark, unit 2.)
5. Missions of the twelve and the seventy, supporting Jesus' ministry. 9: 1–10: 24.
       (Cf. Matthew, parts of units 5, 6; Mark, parts of units 3, 4.)
6. Jesus' great ministry of teaching outside Galilee. 10: 25–19: 28.
       (Here is a collection of many brief illustrations of Jesus' ministry and teaching. The shorter units must sometimes be too short for reading. The reader will readily group them in twos and threes. For this entire unit, compare Matthew, units 2, 4, 7, 8, 9, where much of the same material occurs in different arrangement.)
    a. Friendly relations with men and with God. 10: 25–11: 13.
    b. The Pharisees' lack of spiritual discernment. 11: 14–54.
    c. Encouragement to trust in God even through impending judgment. Ch. 12.
    d. Questionings and answers. Ch 13.
    e. Discourses at table and by the way. Ch. 14.
    f. Parables of grace. Ch. 15.
    g. Parables of warning. Ch. 16.
    h. Forgiveness, faith, and gratitude. 17: 1–19.
    i. The coming of the kingdom. 17: 20–37.
    j. Parables of prayer. 18: 1–14.
    k. Jesus mingling with people. 18: 15–19: 10.
    l. Parable of the pounds. 19: 11–28.

7. Jesus' final ministry in Jerusalem. 19: 29–21: 38.
    (Cf. Matthew, units 7, 8, 9; Mark, units 5, 6, 7.)
8. The passion and crucifixion. Chs. 22, 23.
    (Cf. Matthew, part of unit 10; Mark, part of unit 8.)
9. The resurrection and ascension. Ch. 24.
    (Cf. Matthew, last of unit 10; Mark, last of unit 8.)

John: The Gospel of Jesus' Self-Revelation

Most Bible readers are aware that the Gospel of John stands in a class by itself. The first three, with all their individuality, have much the same general point of view, so that we call them "Synoptic," that is, "seeing together." They place the bulk of Jesus' work in Galilee; they lay stress on his ministry to the peasant classes; they picture him teaching mostly by proverb and parable; they present him as the friend of man. But the Gospel of John, in all but two or three chapters, represents Jesus on frequent tours into Judaea. Here he meets the leaders of the people and engages in constant controversy with them. His teaching is never done by parable, but always through argument. His very healing ministry, while as prominent in John as in the Synoptics, appears most often as the ground of controversy, with little said about his compassion for the sufferers. And the content of his teaching, which, in the first three Gospels, has consisted largely of injunctions for living, becomes in John assertions about his own character, a discussion of his relation to his Father in will and work. Jesus' table talk with his disciples is unique in John. There is much stress on the Holy Spirit, and no discourse on last things.

It is indeed interesting that we have in the Gospel of John so much of the ministry of Jesus that would be unknown but for this one book. Whether the direct authorship is that of John, or whether these interpretations of the Christ come from those who later "saw and heard," it must be that in some way the pictures of the Lord that are here etched in such wondrous fashion stem from him who leaned back on Jesus' breast and partook in a special way of his spirit as the disciple "whom Jesus loved."

Obviously the reading units will have little or no parallel in the Synoptics. Even when the same story does occur, as happens occasionally, it is found in a different setting or with a new interpretation. The chapter divisions are unusually good in this Gospel. The reading may be broken at almost any chapter, though the following units are to be preferred.

1. Introduction. The "Word of God." 1: 1–18.
2. The early ministry in Judaea. 1: 19–2: 22.
3. Interviews with leaders in their communities. 2: 23–4: 54.
    a. With Nicodemus of Jerusalem. 2: 23–3: 36.
    b. With the woman of Samaria and the nobleman of Galilee. Ch. 4.
4. Jesus' oneness with his Father in his will and work. Ch. 5.
5. The Bread of Life come down out of heaven. Ch. 6.
6. Argument with the Jews on Jesus as the light and the great "I am." Chs. 7, 8.
7. Acting and teaching the part of the Good Shepherd. 9: 1–10: 18.
8. The Son of God and the Lord of life. 10: 19–11: 57.
9. Three sources of honor paid to Jesus. Ch. 12.
10. Friends distinguished from foes by menial service. 13: 1–30.
11. Jesus' intimacy with his faithful band. 13: 31–17: 26.
    a. Answering their troubled questions. 13: 31–14: 31.
    b. Establishing them in himself: the vine and the branches. Ch. 15.
    c. Pledging them the Holy Spirit. Ch. 16.
    d. Interceding for them. Ch. 17.
12. The trial and crucifixion of Jesus. Chs. 18, 19.
    (Compare and contrast these scenes in the Synoptics.)
13. The resurrection and the renewal of fellowship. Chs. 20, 21.
    (Compare and contrast with the Synoptics.)

A HARMONY OF THE GOSPELS
BY SHORTER READING UNITS

The practice of "harmonizing" the many parallels in the Gospels is almost as old as the Christian church itself. At times this has developed into a rather vicious habit of trying to force the Gospels into an artificial sameness. Nevertheless, where the right of each to speak for itself is fully recognized, there may be great profit in tracing the outline of the story of Jesus that is common to them.

There are many good harmonies on the market which print in full the texts of the Gospels in parallel columns. It is highly desirable that each Christian family own and use one of these. But for those who do not have one handy the following outline of parallel reading units is constructed so that with nothing more than his Bible the reader may go through the four Gospels together.

Several difficulties are encountered in preparing such a harmony as this. Though the Synoptic Gospels are so alike in many respects, there are two large exceptions to their similarity. For one thing, the Gospel of Matthew does not appear to have the attention to order that is found in Mark and Luke. Matthew's interest is so strongly in what Jesus taught that he is almost indifferent to the arrangement of events. For this reason this table of passages will be following the order in Mark and Luke quite carefully on the whole, and will seem to jump around a great deal in Matthew in order to keep the parallel of thought. The other exception to similarity lies in the Matthew-Luke parallels of the teachings themselves. As has been pointed out, there are many of the teachings of Jesus common to Matthew and Luke which are not in Mark. But in Matthew these are often grouped in longer sermons, while in Luke they are scattered through the narrative of events. In order to be as true as possible to the point of view of each Gospel, these teachings have been listed twice in the following outlines. When we come to the point of Matthew's sermons (usually in the earlier part of the lists) the parallel thought in Luke is enclosed in parentheses. The reader will readily note from how wide a range of chapters in Luke these parallels must be taken. Then when we come to the same teachings in Luke's order, the parallel thoughts in Matthew will be gathered in parentheses.

The Gospel of John, with its different set of events and its varying interpretations of the same events, presents so few real parallels to the Synoptics up to the time of the passion week that the arrangement of its material in the general outline is bound to be somewhat arbitrary.

115

Titles of Reading Units	Matt.	Mark	Luke	John
d. Itinerant preaching and healing	(8: 1–4)	1: 35–2: 12	4: 42–44	
	9: 1–8		5: 12–26	
e. Actions of Jesus causing criticism	9: 9–17	2: 13–3: 6	5: 27–6: 11	
	12: 1–14			
5. The great teaching ministry in Galilee (Matthew's order dominant)				
a. The fame of Jesus	12: 15–21	3: 7–12		
b. Choosing disciples	5: 1–16	3: 13–19	6: 12–19	
c. The blessedness of discipleship			6: 20–26	
d. Greater righteousness required in discipleship than under law	5: 17–48		6: 27–36	
			(12: 58, 59)	
			(16: 18)	
e. Keeping life free from show	6: 1–18		(11: 1–4)	
f. Making life single to God	6: 19–34		(11: 34, 35)	
			(12: 22–34)	
			(16: 13)	
g. The judgment attitude	7: 1–6		6: 37–42	
h. Confidence in asking God	7: 7–11		(11: 9–13)	
i. Kingdom righteousness requires doing	7: 12–29		6: 43–49	
j. Miracles in the midst of teaching	8: 1–13		7: 1–17	
k. Teaching resulting from the message from John	11: 2–30		7: 18–35	
			(10: 12–15, 21, 22)	

116

	Matthew	Mark	Luke	John
l. The devotion of women of Galilee to Jesus				
m. "Spiritual things are spiritually discerned"	(9: 32–34) 12: 22–45	3: 20–30	7: 36–8: 3 (6: 43–45) (11: 14–31) (12: 10)	
n. Jesus' kindred, physical and spiritual	12: 46–50	3: 31–35	8: 19–21	
o. Parables of the kingdom	13: 1–53	4: 1–34	8: 4–18 (13: 18–21)	
6. Jesus' display of mastery				
a. Over the tempest	8: 18, 23–27	4: 35–41	8: 23–25	
b. Over the demoniac mind	8: 28–34	5: 1–20	8: 26–39	
c. Over fear and death	9: 1, 18–26	5: 21–43	8: 40–56	
d. Over blindness and dumbness	9: 27–34			
7. The crisis in Galilee				
a. Jesus rejected	13: 54–58	6: 1–6		
b. The mission and instruction of the twelve	9: 35–11: 1	6: 7–13	9: 1–6	
c. The death of John the Baptist	14: 1–12	6: 14–29	9: 7–9	
d. The feeding of the multitude, with the attempt to make Jesus king	14: 13–23	6: 30–46	9: 10–17	6: 1–15
e. Jesus walking on the water to his disciples	14: 24–36	6: 47–56		6: 16–21
f. Discussion of the Bread of Life				6: 23–71
g. Discussion of true cleanness	15: 1–20	7: 1–23		
8. Jesus and his disciples north and east of Galilee				
a. Experiences in Tyre and Sidon	15: 21–28	7: 24–30		
b. Miracles in Decapolis	15: 29–31	7: 31–37		

	MATT.	MARK	LUKE	JOHN
TITLES OF READING UNITS				
9. *Jesus teaches his disciples the new lesson of the cross*				
a. Back at Lake Galilee	15: 32–16: 12	8: 1–26		
b. Confession of faith at Caesarea Philippi	16: 13–20	8: 27–30	9: 18–21	
c. Jesus explains to the twelve his coming death and resurrection	16: 21–28	8: 31–9: 1	9: 23–27	
d. Jesus transfigured before three disciples	17: 1–13	9: 2–13	9: 28–36	
e. Jesus redeems failure of the other nine	17: 14–21	9: 14–29	9: 37–42	
f. Jesus re-emphasizes his approaching death	17: 22, 23	9: 30–32	9: 43–45	
g. The coin in the fish's mouth	17: 24–27			
10. *The great lesson on humility*	18: 1–35	9: 33–50	9: 46–50	
11. *Some visits to Jerusalem*				
a. Healing the infirm man, with the discussion on the will of God				Ch. 5
b. Excited questioning at the time of the Feast of the Tabernacles				7: 1–52
c. The woman taken in adultery				(7: 53–8: 11)
d. Teaching on the light of the world				8: 12–30
e. Teaching on true freedom				8: 31–59
f. Healing the man born blind				Ch. 9
g. The good Shepherd is the son of God				Ch. 10
12. *Jesus' ministry beyond Galilee (Luke's order dominant)*				
a. Jesus leaves Galilee	19: 1, 2	10: 1	9: 51–56	

118

119

121

TITLES OF READING UNITS	MATT.	MARK	LUKE	JOHN
e. A lesson in menial service			22: 24–27	13: 1–20
f. The Love Feast, with the revelation of the traitor				13: 21–38
g. Jesus reassures his own				Ch. 14
h. Abiding in friendship with Jesus				Ch. 15
i. The promise of the Spirit and of power				Ch. 16
j. Jesus prays for his own				Ch. 17
16. The humiliation of Jesus				
a. The Olivet agony	26: 36–46	14: 32–42	22: 39–46	
b. The betrayal and arrest	26: 47–56	14: 43–52	22: 47–53	18: 1–12
c. The ecclesiastical trials of Jesus, with Peter's denials	26: 57–75	14: 53–72	22: 54–71	18: 12–27
d. The civil trials of Jesus, with the mockery	27: 1, 2, 11–31	15: 1–20	23: 1–25	18: 28–19:16
e. The fate of the traitor	27: 3–10			
f. The crucifixion	27: 32–56	15: 21–41	23: 26–49	19: 17–37
g. The burial, and the guard at the tomb	27: 57–66	15: 42–47	23: 50–56	19: 38–42
17. The exaltation of Jesus				
a. The resurrection morn	28: 1–15	16: 1–8	24: 1–12	20: 1–18
b. Resurrection evening, and a week later			24: 13–43	20: 19–29
c. Final meeting by the old fishing grounds				21: 1–24
d. The mountain-top and the ascension	28: 16–20		24: 44–53	
The epilogue to the gospel				20: 30, 31
				21: 25

122

THE ACTS OF THE APOSTLES:
UNITS OF CHURCH EXPANSION

The importance of the book of Acts can hardly be overstated. A religious history, written with all the devotion to facts that any realist could desire, but with a spiritual enthusiasm that surpasses that of the Old Testament chronicler, this work traces the doings of the apostles of the early church. The writer had learned well from the historical books of the Hebrews that sacred history is best written by describing the activity of God in the lives of its great motivators. Therefore Peter and John and Philip and Paul with a host of lesser lights are the centers of interest in this dramatic story, not the changing forms of the church. To be sure we see the struggles, the fears and hopes, the plans and aggressiveness of the Christian community, but we see them in terms of the determined course which the leaders took. The fervent devotion, the daring endurance, the missionary zeal, are not matters of statistical reports, but of the glowing passions of those who threw their lives away for their Christ. It was because men had been set upon by the grace and power of God that they could not keep from proclaiming the gospel. As Peter and John expressed it, "We cannot but speak of what we have seen and heard" (4: 20).

The early church centered its faith in Jesus as Lord (10: 36). It had indeed many beliefs and practices in common with the Jews— worship at the temple and in the synagogues, use of the Old Testament, preaching to Jews first. But it was from the beginning a community to itself, caring for its own, eating and worshiping together (1: 12–14; 2: 44–47).

It must not be supposed that the early church found it easy to arrive at its full faith, much less to proclaim it. The Christians at Samaria had to be brought from a baptism of water to a full baptism of the Holy Spirit (ch. 8). Paul had to discover that even a sincere following of the law was not enough and he had to experience a radical conversion to Christ (ch. 9). Even Peter, follower of Jesus though he was, had to be brought from a racial pride to see that

Jesus could make brothers of all men (ch. 10). The church itself had to learn by degrees that the way of conference is infinitely superior to controversy (chs. 11, 15).

In all this growth from "babes in Christ" to mature men of faith, the Holy Spirit was the great leader of the church. It has well been said that this book should be called, not "The Acts of the Apostles," but "The Acts of the Holy Spirit." It will amaze the reader the number of times the Spirit is named as the real doer of a deed or the instigator of a faith. The variety of interests and actions attributed to the Spirit runs all the way from inspiring prayer to directing men where to go, from selecting missionaries to killing deceivers. From Pentecost to Paul's rescue from shipwreck, the Holy Spirit is the real Person of the book of Acts.

The following reading units are suggested:

1. Early popularity of the Christians in Jerusalem. Chs. 1–3.
   a. The historical background. Ch. 1.
   b. The Pentecostal experience. Ch.2.
   c. The healing at the temple gate. Ch. 3.
2. Opposition from without and treachery from within. Chs. 4, 5.
   a. The Sadducees resent the stress on the resurrection. 4: 1–22.
   b. The beautiful unity of the Christians. 4: 23–37.
   c. Treachery meets immediate disaster. 5: 1–14.
   d. The priests oppose the apostles. 5: 14–42.
3. "The blood of the martyrs is the seed of the church." Chs. 6–8.
   a. Helpers for the apostles. 6: 1–7.
   b. Activities of Stephen leading to his martyrdom. 6: 8–7: 60.
   c. The apostles, scattered abroad, preach the word. Ch. 8.
4. Two leaders experience change of heart, Chs. 9, 10.
   a. The experience of Saul on the Damascus road. Ch. 9.
   b. The experience of Peter at Joppa and Caesarea. Ch. 10.
5. Co-operation amid growing persecution. Chs. 11, 12.
   a. A Christian conference at Jerusalem. Ch. 11.
   b. Peter escapes the intrigues of Herod. Ch. 12.
6. The mission of the Antioch church. Chs. 13, 14.
7. The conference method used again. 15: 1–35.
8. Paul's great mission to Macedonia and Achaia. 15: 36–18: 28.
   a. Paul in Galatia and Macedonia. 15: 36–17: 15.
   b. Paul in Achaia. 17: 16–18: 28.

9. Paul's ministry in and near Ephesus. Chs. 19, 20.
10. Paul's arrest in Jerusalem and preliminary hearing. 21: 1–22: 29.
11. Paul's trials in Jerusalem and in Caesarea. 22: 30–26: 32.
    a. The Sanhedrin trial leads to Paul's removal to Caesarea. 22: 30–23: 35.
    b. The trial before Felix. Ch. 24.
    c. The trial before Festus. Ch. 25.
    d. The trial before Agrippa. Ch. 26.
12. Paul goes to Rome. Chs. 27, 28.
    a. The journey and shipwreck. Ch. 27.
    b. From the island of rescue to the capital. Ch. 28.

READING PAUL'S LETTERS WITH THE BOOK OF ACTS

The Apostle Paul was, in the best sense of the word, a "practical man." While he was a great dreamer and a great student of the purpose and plan of God, he did not develop his dreams and studies in theoretical fashion. He was a doer of heroic deeds, a traveler and preacher of the cross of Christ. It is unlikely that he ever would have put pen to papyrus on the subject of his religion had he been able to be continuously with the many churches he carried on his heart. But the necessity of frequent absence deepened his sense of responsibility for the problems he learned were arising in their midst. So he tried to meet his responsibility by writing to each congregation about those problems. How well he succeeded, the early church attested by gathering his letters together and adding them to the Gospels in the making of our New Testament. The church of all ages has gone back to them again and again as examples of inspired literature dealing by principles that are everlasting with types of needs that are to be met over and over.

The book of the Acts, in its descriptions of Paul's travels among many of the churches to which he later wrote, furnishes us with a background for understanding these letters. It will prove valuable to read them at times in connection with the appropriate chapters in Acts. But it must be kept in mind that reading in this way will mean to disregard the order in which the letters were written.

The letter to the Galatians has very rich support from the book of Acts. Unit 6 of our outline of Acts (chapters 13 and 14) describes Paul's missionary tour, the major part of which was spent among the Galatian churches. The events are suggestive of the warm reception but later fickle dealing of these people as we find them pictured in the letter to the Galatians. Unit 7 of Acts (most of chapter 15) describes the Jerusalem conference which is probably the same as that of the second chapter of Galatians. To read Acts 13–15 with Galatians, then, is to correlate the two in a most illuminating way.

Unit 8,a of our reading outline of Acts takes us with Paul into his experiences in Macedonia. Here from 16: 1–17: 15 we trace the rapid progress of the first mission in Europe. To two of the cities described here Paul later wrote, to Philippi and to Thessalonica. His two letters to the Thessalonians were written from Corinth, only a few months after the visits pictured in the Acts. Close reading of these letters with these paragraphs from the Acts will reveal something of the anxiety in the midst of persecution which is their deepest trouble. The letter to the Philippians was written long after, when Paul was a prisoner, probably in Rome, yet even here the account of the early ministry in Philippi will help set the stage for the reading of this kindliest of all Paul's writings.

Unit 8,b describes Paul in Athens and Corinth. The entire 18th chapter of Acts is given to a narrative of events in Corinth. It will be well worth reading in connection with Paul's two important letters to the Corinthians, especially with the first.

Unit 9 (Acts, chapters 19 and 20) describes Paul's two- or three-year stay in and around Ephesus. Here he not only taught and preached in the great city of Ephesus itself, but he sent out many evangelistic expeditions to various parts of Asia Minor. We are reasonably sure that the church at Colossae was founded during this period, though Paul probably did not visit it himself. Therefore, in connection with these two chapters of Acts, the two quite similar letters, Ephesians and Colossians, should be read. The fight against idolatry is noteworthy in both the letters and the Acts. Also at this point may be read the little letter to Philemon, who was a leading member of the Colossian church. These three letters were all written from Paul's imprisonment somewhere near the same time as his letter to the Philippians.

Finally, the great Letter to the Romans may well be read with the closing sections of the book of Acts. Chapters 21–28 describe Paul's repeated trials by Jewish and Roman officials and his eventful trip to Rome itself, ending with a picture of his ministry there as a prisoner. The letter to the Romans was written ahead of this trip.

The pastoral writings that bear Paul's name, I and II Timothy and Titus, were addressed to situations which arose later than the history that is told in the book of Acts. Hence they cannot be related to any part of the narrative.

ROMANS: UNITS OF THE DOCTRINE OF SALVATION

We have said that Paul did not plan for his writings any system of doctrinal teachings, but that he penned his instruction in reply to specific needs that arose in the various churches. But in his Letter to the Romans, who lived in the great capital of the empire, he took occasion to draw up for a church he had not yet seen the whole scheme of salvation in Christ as he understood it. Here Paul glories in the death of Christ, and explains life by it. He traces the sin of man, the righteousness of God, the redemption that is in Christ, the life of faith, the growth in grace, and the meaning of Christian discipleship within the church and the state. As a Jewish patriot of the first rank he is deeply concerned about his own people and he devotes a special section to the consideration of their privileges, their failure, and his hope of their final redemption. This letter should be read, then, in units that mark the various steps of progress from spiritual death to spiritual life. Again, the longer units are strongly recommended in order to get the train of thought clear, but the shorter units are suggested for those who feel they must divide the reading.

1. The guilt of Gentile and Jew alike has made necessary the death of Christ. Chs. 1–3.
   a. The guilt of the Gentile world. Ch. 1.
   b. The guilt of the Jewish world. 2: 1–3: 20.
   c. The righteousness of God in the death of Christ. 3: 21–31.

2. The blessings of faith. Chs. 4, 5.
   a. The faith of old, as seen in Abraham. Ch. 4.
   b. The faith of the Christian in Christ the second Adam. Ch. 5.
3. Growth in grace toward triumphant living. Chs. 6–8.
   a. The imperative to be free from sin. 6: 1–7: 6.
   b. The difficulty of being free from sin. 7: 7–25.
   c. The glorious achievement of freedom in Christ. Ch. 8.
4. The question of the Jew's special privilege. Chs. 9–11.
   a. The absolute freedom of God seen in his various choosings within the families of men. Ch. 9.
   b. The Jews' rejection of God's choice of them is their own responsibility. Ch. 10.
   c. God's subsequent choice of the Gentiles may provoke the Jews to final acceptance. Ch. 11.
5. Questions of practical Christian living. Chs. 12–16.
   a. The principle of the living sacrifice. Ch. 12.
   b. The principle of subjection in love. Chs. 13, 14.
   c. Matters personal to Paul and the Romans. Chs. 15, 16.

I CORINTHIANS: UNITS OF CHURCH PROBLEMS

In reading Paul's first letter to the Corinthians every modern church worker should feel at home. Indeed, for one who is unacquainted with Paul, this is rather a good place to begin. His method has already been pointed out in chapter 4 under "Story Units of Problems." Here Paul spends his time discussing very real issues in the life of a very real church in a way calculated to solve them. The actual problems have mostly passed, but the types which they represent are with us still. The particular things Paul said to do with those who lived lives of incest in the church, with those who frequented idols' temples, with those women who would not keep the veil, have no bearing on our situations. But the problems of misusing freedom, of thoughtless example, and of lack of modesty, which they illustrate, are ever our own.

Paul does not content himself with trying to change a passing situation. In each case he seeks to show the eternal principle of Christian living which is involved. This is what makes this letter so profoundly interesting and so continually up to date. The reader must seek to see the relation of eternal principle to immediate problem in each of the following units.

1. The preaching of the cross solves problems of personalities. Chs. 1–4.
     (Should not be broken.)
2. Putting others before self meets problems of personal morals and of strife. Chs. 5–7.
     a. The problem of licentiousness. 5: 1–13; 6: 12–20.
     b. The problem of lawsuits. 6: 1–11.
     c. The problem of marriage in a day of persecution. Ch. 7.
3. Putting others before self meets problems of fellowship and of influence. Chs. 8–11.
     a. The question of fellowship at the idols' temple. 8: 1–11: 1.
        (Should not be broken for best results.)
     b. The question of the fellowship of the sexes in worship. 11: 2–16.
     c. The question of social fellowship at the Lord's table. 11: 17–34.
4. Love binds together all spiritual gifts, ensuring their usefulness. Chs. 12–14.
     a. The variety of spiritual gifts in the church. Ch. 12.
     b. The law of love in the use of all gifts. Ch. 13.
     c. The relative merits of various gifts. Ch. 14.
5. The reality of Christ's resurrection solves the problem of ours. Ch. 15.
6. Matters personal. Ch. 16.

II CORINTHIANS: UNITS OF PERSONAL MINISTRY

The second letter to the Corinthians is somewhat confusing to read. Its subject matters are not so closely related as those in Paul's other letters. The spirit and mood change decidedly as between the first few chapters and the last four. The early portions are quite conciliatory in tone, as though Paul realized he had hurt his readers. The later chapters, however, include a vicious attack on Paul's enemies. Some feel that the letter may be made up of various bits of correspondence. Throughout there is a moodiness which sometimes characterized Paul. But the letter is noteworthy for its majestic description of the glories of the ministry, for its clear annunciation of the principles of benevolent giving, and for its taking aside the veil from the heart of a naturally shy man and letting us see some of his most private experiences with Christ.

1. Paul's analysis of the Christian ministry. Chs. 1–7.
   a. Paul's justification of his own ministry. Chs. 1, 2.
   b. The glorious Christian ministry surpasses the glories of all other ministry. 3: 1–6: 10.
      (A wonderful passage, that should not be broken in reading.)
   c. Paul's recollections of his own ministry in Macedonia and Achaia. 6: 11–7: 16.
2. Ministry through an offering for the suffering Jewish Christians. Chs. 8, 9.
3. Paul's experience with God justifies his ministry, in spite of all his foes. Chs. 10–13.

Galatians: A Unit of Fiery Defense of the Gospel

This is Paul's most vigorous letter. It is the only one in which he does not stop to praise his readers. He had given the first-fruits of his ministry to Galatia, only to be followed there by whisperers who attempted to persuade the people that he was not really an apostle and who sought return to the dictates of the Jewish law. Paul is determined that nothing shall interfere with the freedom that faith brings. Especially is he valiant in the defense of that freedom for Gentile believers so that they may not be forced to become Jews. He shows that faith will produce a moral life that can be trusted far more readily than the enjoined morality of commandments. While the letter is a unit, as noted in chapter 2, it falls rather neatly into three parts, dealing with the three subjects just noted.

1. Paul's defense of his apostleship. Chs. 1, 2.
2. Paul's defense of the gospel of faith. Chs. 3, 4.
3. Paul's defense of the morality of faith. Chs. 5, 6.

Ephesians: Units of the Headship of Christ

We often speak of Ephesians, Colossians, and Philippians as the "Christological Epistles," because of their enthronement of the person of Christ. The similarity between the first two has already been pointed out. Each falls into two nearly equal parts, the first of which treats the theme of the headship of Christ, the second the application of this theme to everyday living, particularly in the family. In the case of Ephesians, special stress is laid on the headship of Christ in the church. This letter is beautiful in its mellow grace, and is full of lovely figures.

1. Christ the center of all God's grace. Chs. 1–3.
    a. God's gracious foreordination of Christ to be the Savior of mankind. 1: 1–2: 10.
    b. Gentile as well as Jew included in this grace. 2:11–21.
    c. The rich spiritual blessings of this grace. Ch. 3.
2. The headship of Christ applied to Christian living. Chs. 4–6.
    a. To the church. 4: 1–16.
    b. To morality. 4: 17–5: 14.
    c. To family relationships. 5: 15–6: 9.
    d. To the struggles of life. 6: 10–23.

PHILIPPIANS: A UNIT OF STUDY OF THE MIND OF CHRIST

This is Paul's tenderest letter. Moved by the gift from the Philippian Christians to the needs of his prison experience, he writes to assure them of his love for this church, "his joy and crown." He seeks to allay their fears about the furtherance of his ministry, emphasizing the joy that comes in finding all possible ways of serving Christ.

The inspired passage on the mind of Christ, 2: 5–11, suggests a touchstone for the whole of this little letter. It can scarcely be divided into reading units, for it is a love letter, glowing with warm feeling. It is an emotion, not an argument. It is a gracious touching on many of the heartstrings of life where the having of the mind of Christ will keep life joyful in the midst of pain and hindrance, aggressive in the midst of limited opportunity, triumphant in the face of outward failure.

Colossians: A Unit of the Headship of Christ

In the letter to the Colossians much stress is laid on the headship of Christ over the physical universe. Paul had met with philosophers of the day who were interested in cosmic theories that would not allow so good a head as Christ to be associated with the creation of what they deemed an evil world.

The letter may appropriately be read at one sitting, though, like Ephesians, it may be broken in two around thesis and application.

1. The headship of Christ over all creation. 1: 1–2: 15.
2. Applying the headship of Christ to living. 2: 16–4: 18.
    a. To problems of moral renewal. 2: 16–3: 17.
    b. To family relationships. 3: 18–4: 1.
    c. To relationships with Paul and others. 4: 2–18.

I Thessalonians: A Unit in Exhortation

The Thessalonian letters are among Paul's earliest writings. They display his earnestness in general exhortation.

To suggest divisions for such a letter as I Thessalonians is but to invite the reader to stop reading where he should go on. This is not a closely reasoned writing, such as Galatians or Ephesians or Colossians among the shorter ones. Its style is somewhat discursive. Here Paul intermingles his thought of the people's fear in the face of rising persecution, of anxious impatience over the delayed return of the Lord, and of laxity in morals. The tone is mild.

II Thessalonians: A Unit in Explanation

Even the Apostle Paul was not always understood when he wrote a letter! The reader who has had the embarrassing experience of finding that something he wrote to a friend was misinterpreted can sympathize with Paul. He had sought to comfort his readers in the preceding letter with the assurance that Christ would soon come and put an end to their troubles. But they took this as an excuse to relax, waiting for Christ to do what they should have been doing.

The tone of this second letter is one of sharp rebuke, explaining that the coming of Christ is by no means so soon as they anticipate, and urging active service if they are to be ready for that coming.

I TIMOTHY: A UNIT OF MINISTERIAL TRAINING

I and II Timothy and Titus, called "Pastoral Epistles" because written to pastors, bear in our New Testament the name of Paul. We have noted that there is no place for them to fit in the story of the book of Acts. That story ends with Paul in prison at Rome, apparently hoping for release. The Letter to the Philippians breathes Paul's earnest expectation that he will get free. There is nothing in the New Testament to tell us whether his expectation was realized or not. But some of the early church fathers say that it was, and that he went on another long missionary journey before being arrested again and suffering martyrdom. If this is correct, it would account adequately for the pastorals as letters of Paul. According to them Paul established Timothy at Ephesus and then wrote him two letters from prison. He established Titus on the island of Crete and wrote to him.

Like I Thessalonians, the First Letter to Timothy is not a logical development of thought, but a discursive treatment of what the church requires of its members, what kind of people ought to be made church officers, and how the younger minister, Timothy, should personally conduct himself. There is no logical way of dividing this reading unit. The letter is brief enough to be read as one, though stopping at any chapter will not be destructive of value in this case. The letter contains what is perhaps the oldest known stanza of a Christian hymn, the words being also a confession of faith (3: 16).

II TIMOTHY: A UNIT OF VALEDICTORY ADDRESS

The Second Letter to Timothy differs considerably from the first. It breathes the spirit of the ancient martyrs, "We who are about to die salute you." It is an aged saint's valedictory. He knows now that he cannot escape execution. He pours out his soul to his favorite, Timothy, glorying in his own ministry and pleading for the full performance of Timothy's. There is pathos in the appeal of this letter, sadness and yet the beauty of triumphant joy.

Titus: A Unit of Ministerial Duty

This letter is very similar to I Timothy, consisting of instructions to Titus in still briefer form for establishment of the church in the difficult environment of Crete.

Philemon: Paul's Graciousness at Its Best

This leaf from Paul's career is beloved of all Christians for its concern for a runaway slave in the form of a cordial appeal to his master. The delicate grace of this plea is worthy of the most refined follower of Jesus. Its assumption of responsibility is characteristic of the courage of its author. Its assumption that the wealthy Philemon, because he is a Christian friend of Paul, will receive his slave back "as a beloved brother" is the undercutting of all slavery, a far more effective approach to dealing with an evil institution than sermonic denunciation would have been.

Hebrews: Units of Superiority
of the New over the Old

The Letter to the Hebrews was apparently written to those Jewish Christians who had lost the first flush of their new faith and were in danger of going back to the old because of its attractive history and forms. The letter is an appeal to steadfast loyalty to Jesus as supreme over all the blessings which the old religion offered. The author's method is not to degrade the old, but to take it at its best, in its leading characters, its beauty of worship, its covenant, its priesthood, its offering, its access to God, and then to show that in each case the Christian faith has that which is better. The reading units, therefore, are these comparisons between new and old. The letter is written in elegance and restraint of style, and yet is warm with frequent exhortations to lay hold of our superior salvation.

1. Jesus the better minister. 1: 1–4: 13.
   a. Better than the angels of the old dispensation. Chs. 1, 2.
   b. Better than Moses, the deliverer. Ch. 3.
   c. Better than David and Joshua. 4: 1–13.
2. Jesus the better priest. 4: 14–7: 28.
   a. Better than the lineal priests from Aaron. 4: 14–6: 20.
   b. Better than Melchizedek, the priest of character. Ch. 7.
3. Jesus the mediator of a better convenant. 8: 1–10: 18.
   a. His new covenant, as Jeremiah predicted, is written on the heart. Ch. 8.
   b. His covenant secures real access to God where the old and its priests failed. 9: 1–10: 18.
4. Exhortations to faith and love in following Jesus. 10: 19–13: 25.
   a. Faith ensures steadfastness of following. 10: 19–12: 13.
   b. Love of the brethren ensures peace. 12: 14–13: 25.

JAMES: A UNIT IN CHRISTIAN LIVING

The letter of James to the church at large is the first of the group called the "Catholic, or General, Epistles," because they were written to no one church in particular but to Christians everywhere. They include the remainder of the New Testament save for the last book. James, as a book of wisdom, carries its thought beyond the point of view of the Old Testament. For example, whereas in the book of Proverbs the ability to speak well is highly praised, James warns against the overuse or misuse of speech (3: 1–5); and though in the Old Testament "Wisdom" is usually thought of as either possessed or fatally lacking, James teaches that a man who lacks wisdom can get it by asking from God (1: 5).

This little letter of James is an early Christian homily in the style of the Proverbs. Like the earlier book it has unit proverbs (the single couplet) and clusters of proverbs around some theme. The popular themes in James are temptation, the relation of the rich and poor, the use of the tongue, the relation of faith to deeds, and of faith to healing. Most of these themes are treated more than once. There is, however, no order of arrangement in James' treatment of his many subjects but the same themes recur in cycles. The letter should be read as one, but note may be made of the cycles beginning at 1: 1, 1: 5, 1: 12, 1: 19, 2: 1, 2: 14, 3: 1, 3: 13, 4: 1, 4: 13, 5: 1, 5: 7, 5: 13.

I Peter: A Unit Study in Christian Suffering

The question asked in the dramatic debate between Job and his friends, and left unanswered there, finds its satisfaction not in the solving of a curiosity problem but in the searching thought of this letter. Why do the righteous suffer? Such a question carries the mood of complaint. Peter changes this into a mood of deep joy so as to make it read, How may the righteous suffer? The kind of suffering he deals with is that resulting from misinterpretation and persecution because of righteousness. Peter says that God has suffered for this, and the Christian who shares such suffering thereby seals his membership in the family of God.

1. The privileges of the Christian sufferer. 1: 1–2: 10.
2. The duties of the Christian sufferer. 2: 11–4: 11.
3. The trials of the Christian sufferer. 4: 12–5: 14.

II Peter: A Unit of Warning Against False Teachers

The main purpose of II Peter is to warn Christian disciples against false teachers who have arisen within the church. It is noteworthy that the writer is not concerned with those who teach some false theory or interpretation, but with those whose teaching is of such a nature as to result in bad living. His fiery denunciation of these teachers is matched by his expectation of the end of the world that is to come with blazing fire. The letter should be read as a unit.

I John: A Unit in the Knowledge
and Love of God

This remarkable little letter bears some points of similarity to that of James. Both are proverbial in their thought and both treat their subjects in cycles. I John is by far the deeper of the two, however, and needs much closer study. The main themes of its cycles are four: the need of Christian love that flows from the love of God, the need of an absolute ethic, the need of reality in belief, and the need of a knowledge of God that is sure. The occasion for these themes was the writer's long acquaintance with a type of religious philosophy that sought to treat as unreal the human nature of Jesus, human suffering that would call for sympathy and love, and selfish living that the Christian knows as sin. This philosophy had its pride of knowledge which John seeks to meet with true spiritual knowledge.

As in the case of other proverb cycles, we cannot outline units of reading, but can only point to the places where the themes recur. These points are: 1: 1, 1: 5, 2: 7, 2: 18, 2: 29, 3: 13, 4: 1, 4: 7, 5: 1, 5: 13. If the reading of the letter must be broken, this will best be done at 2: 18 or at chapter 3 or chapter 4.

II John: A Note of Affection

This little note of John to "the elect lady" affectionately greets a friend and encourages her about her children. It may be that John meant to spiritualize the recipient into a church and its members.

III John: A Note of Gratitude

To another friend John writes in gratitude for his show of hospitality to itinerant preachers of the faith who were traveling in Asia Minor. Some there were who were not only failing to practice, but were actually forbidding, hospitality to these Christian strangers. So hard has it always been to open the home and the heart!

Jude: A Unit of Warning Against
False Teachers

The relation of this brief writing to II Peter is apparent to anyone who reads both. In fact, the reading of Jude should precede the
reading of II Peter. The purpose of the two is the same: to warn
against false teachers in the church. The language is largely the same,
the denunciation stinging. Jude, however, contains a beautiful benediction.

Revelation: Units of Vision
of the Triumphant Christ

The book of Revelation is a closed writing to many Christians.
It is thought of as a hidden mystery. But it is meant to be, what its
name suggests, a revealing. So it was to the Christians who first read
it. So it would be to us if we would put ourselves into the thought
forms which they used. Apocalyptic as a type of literature will be
explained in chapter 11. Here we may note that the theology of this
great vision is that Christ comes again and again in judgment, both
upon his church and upon the world, that he will protect through
the severest suffering those who are true to his kingdom, and that
he will ultimately bring triumph for righteousness in the new heaven
and the new earth. Cycles appear again, this time numbered by
sevens. Most of the figures that make up these cycles are to be
found in the beautiful and important fourth and fifth chapters
where the worship of God and of the Lamb is magnificently portrayed. As with Daniel, a good commentary is needful.

The following reading units are suggested:

1. The Son of man in the midst of the seven churches. Chs. 1–3.
   a. The vision of the Son of man. Ch. 1.
   b. The description of the churches in terms of his character. Chs.
      2, 3.
2. Worship in heaven. Chs. 4, 5.
   a. The worship of God as Creator. Ch. 4.
   b. The worship of God as Redeemer. Ch. 5.

3. The cycle of the seven seals. Chs. 6, 7.
   a. The first six seals. Ch. 6.
   b. The sealing of the redeemed. Ch. 7.
4. The cycle of the seven trumpets. Chs. 8–11.
   a. The first six trumpets. Chs. 8, 9.
   b. The book of judgment and the faithful witnesses. Chs. 10, 11.
5. The cycle of the seven mystic signs. Chs. 12–14.
   a. The beasts and the offspring of the woman. Chs. 12, 13.
   b. The Lamb and his following. Ch. 14.
6. The cycle of the seven bowls. Chs. 15, 16.
7. The judgment on the harlot city. Chs. 17, 18.
8. The finality of judgment. Chs. 19, 20.
9. The new world order. Chs. 21, 22.

Chapter 9

THE BIBLE AND LIFE'S EXPERIENCES

The last two chapters have centered in the books of the Bible as books. The reading units listed there can be looked upon as so much material, so many lumped passages. But if this is the reaction then the purpose of those lists is lost, for it is never any real accomplishment to read such and such a quantity and cover this or that amount of ground. The earlier chapters of this book have tried to make clear that the Bible is not a mass of apothegms or a compilation of instructions and doctrines, but a living, vivid experiencing of life under the guidance of the Spirit of God. It is not enough that we have "precept upon precept, precept upon precept, line upon line, line upon line" (Isa. 28: 10) in wearying array, but that we are able to follow incident and illustration from the lives of very real people.

Our century has witnessed the coining of such phrases as "pupil-centered" and "experience-centered" in reference to teaching. Whatever may be the limitations of such terms, they at least emphasize that truth is not handed down to rising generations as a finished commodity but must be relived in terms of the new life of each successive generation. The Bible is the original source book for whatever there is of value in experience-centered teaching. Both Old Testament and New contain little formal or codified religion. But they reveal case after case of God's effort to get men to learn by interpreting to them the daily happenings of their lives. Many an Abraham must have left the home of his ancestors without ever learning the lesson of faith, but the hero of faith in the Bible committed his way to God and discovered the revolutionizing truth

140

that God could go with him into paths unknown. It was in learning this that he became the "friend of God." Yet complete as this experience was in the career of the patriarch, Abraham could pass on to his descendants only the knowledge that it had really occurred. His grandson Jacob, for example, had to discover for himself in painful travail that God was not only the God of his fathers, but that he was truly in the place where Jacob was alone, even though he had not known it (Gen. 28: 16). In similar fashion Paul could write to Timothy that he thanked God not only for the faith "that dwelt first in your grandmother Lois and your mother Eunice" but also for the fact that it "dwells in you" (II Tim. 1: 5). Timothy's experiences in company with Paul from Lystra on to the frontier and back to Ephesus had made real to him what he had learned in his home.

The Bible is full of the balance of two ways of learning. The famous passage in Deuteronomy 6 about teaching the truths of religion diligently to the children has always to be checked by the observance that the children must learn for themselves. Our heritage is rich and basic, but our religious faith can only be our own.

Most of us have realized this is one way or another, but we have not been quick to see its application to the spirit in which we should use our Bibles. We have all too often gone to the Book of books in some hour of felt need expecting to find there a program of belief or action all mapped out for us. We have perhaps turned away in disappointment after serious search, saying, "It just doesn't tell me what to do or what to think." Of course not! David and Hosea, Peter and John were not told arbitrarily what to do or what to think. They learned by putting their religion to the acid test of life in the midst of perplexities. Their problems were as real as ours, as difficult, as new. The Bible presents us always with flesh-and-blood people; no mythological Beowulfs fighting symbolic monsters of the sea, but "men, of like nature with you" (Acts 14: 15). Our environment is dressed in modern garments, theirs in ancient; we must face our own day in our own way. But the great value of the Bible to experience is not that it tells us to do as they did, but that it gives great illustrations of how men and women reacted under the guidance of God. There is guidance for us, not so much in seeing what they thought and did, but how, in what spirit, with what motives, with what success or failure they lived their lives. We honor the men of the past, not by keeping their achievements unaltered, but by giving to our own tasks the courage and confidence in God that we see to have been in them. "Consider the outcome of their life, and imitate their faith" (Heb. 13: 7).

We would heartily commend, then, the studying of the life experiences of the great characters of the Bible. We have many printed helps to do this in connection with some particular experience of our own. Some advise us, "When in sorrow read such and such a chapter; when in trouble, or in doubt, or in temptation, or in some other special condition, turn to this or that place in the Bible." Such help is no doubt good, yet it often is but an artificial effort to fit a passage to a mood, forgetting that moods vary with individuals. It easily becomes arbitrary, and may even smack of the dangers of studying the Bible by topics (see ch. 2). It is important to see the spirit and fruits of the lives that God's covenant people have lived rather than seeking for happenings that correspond exactly with our own.

It is tempting to draw up a fairly long list of outstanding experiences of Bible characters. How did they face the consciousness of sin? How did they meet the call of duty? How did they make friends? But such a procedure would tend to take experiences apart and look at them piecemeal rather than to see them as a whole. It may be wise to limit ourselves to two categories: experiences with God, and those with men.

Great Experiences with God

The men and women of the Bible met sin and forgiveness, doubt and faith, trouble and release, as they met God. To see them in their new discoveries of what God is like, to see them as God reveals himself to them in some new character, is to learn how they grew in spiritual living. Here are some of the great biblical cases of experience with God.

Abraham:	After Ishmael's birth, Gen. 17.
	When Isaac seems about to be taken, Gen. 22.
Jacob:	When he is leaving home, Gen. 28.
	When he is returning home, Gen. 32.
Moses:	At the burning bush, Ex. 3.
	With God in the mount and in the tent of meeting, Ex. 32: 1–34: 9.
	After a life of full experience, Psa. 90 (attributed to Moses).
Samuel:	In his childhood, I Sam. 3.
David:	After his sin, Psa. 51 (attributed to David).
	After he found he could not build the temple of his dreams, II Sam. 7.
Elijah:	After his mortifying flight, I Kings 19.
Hezekiah:	When the enemy was at the city walls, II Kings 18, 19.
Job:	After human argument had failed, Job 38–42.
Psalmists:	Most of the Psalms in units 3 and 7 of the reading outlines in chapter 7. Others will be found, especially in units 5 and 6.
Isaiah:	After his disillusionment over King Uzziah, Isa. 6.
Jeremiah:	When he questioned whether even God could make Judah over, Jer. 18.
	When all hope seemed gone, Jer. 32.
Ezekiel:	At his call to ministry, Ezek. 2, 3.
Hosea:	In his domestic tragedy, Hos. 1–3, with 11.
Jonah:	In his call to his work, Jonah, entire.
Habakkuk:	In his repeated efforts to preach, Hab., entire.
Jesus:	At his call to his ministry, Matt. 3: 13–17.
	In his desert temptation, Luke 4: 1–13.
	In his need for choosing disciples, Luke 6: 12–19.
	In the agony of struggle with his will, Luke 22: 39–46.
Paul:	In his conversion, Acts 9 with Gal. 1.
	In the inner fight that Christ resolves, Rom., 7, 8.
	In his mystical visions, II Cor. 12: 1–10.
Peter:	In his restoration to discipleship, John 21.
	In his break in prejudice, Acts 10.
John:	In his exile from his ministry, Rev. 1.

Note in these great unveilings of the hearts of men how often the new revelation of God came when all hope was gone, when failure had brought a sense of worthlessness of self and even of life, or when some impossible task lay ahead. In one way or another these men are our contemporaries in discovering the assurance from God, "My grace is sufficient for you."

In studying biblical experiences of God, it may also be good to read carefully some of the great confessions of faith in God. If the negative of doubt and fear frequently lay behind a rich experience, the experience itself often issued in the positive of a ringing declaration of confidence. Here are some of the outstanding expressions of faith, many of them in situations where great courage was required to speak of God at all—courage which the same speakers had been far from possessing until they had come to know God really.

Joseph:	When brought to interpret Pharaoh's dream, Gen. 40.
Moses:	When facing the dread Pharaoh, Ex. 7, 8.
Samuel:	In his review of his life and convictions, I Sam. 12.
David:	In Psalm 23 and many others.
Solomon:	In his prayer of dedication of the temple, I Kings 8.
Hezekiah:	Before the people at Sennacherib's invasion, Isa. 36, 37.
Isaiah:	Before the people who feared God was not strong, Isa. 40, 41.
Jeremiah:	Expressing faith in the redemption of God, Jer. 31.
Ezekiel:	Proclaiming faith in the regenerative power of God, Ezek. 37.
Hosea:	Proclaiming faith in God's healing power, Hos. 14.
Micah:	Teaching people to look for the coming of good "latter days" from God, Micah 4.
Habakkuk:	In thanksgiving for God when material blessings were gone, Hab. 3.
Daniel:	Before the heathen king, Dan. 6.
Jesus:	In his answers to the tempter, Matt. 4: 1–11.
	In his trial, John 18.
	In his death, Luke 23: 33–49.
Peter:	At Caesarea, Matt. 16: 13–28.
John and Peter:	Before the Sanhedrin, Acts 3.
Stephen:	At his trial, Acts 7.

Isaiah's vision of Israel worshiping with the hated Egyptians and
Assyrians. Isa. 19: 19–25.

The inclusion of an enemy Moabite in the lineage of David. Ruth
4: 13–22.

The emphasis on God's love for pagan Nineveh. Jonah 3, 4.

Jesus' repeated dwelling on the good in unlikely people, especially
the despised race of the Samaritans. Mark 7: 24–30; Luke 4: 24–30;
7: 2–10; 10: 30–37; 17: 11–19; John 4.

Jesus' prayer that his followers might all be one. John 17.

Peter's discovery that no man is unclean. Acts 10.

Paul's insistence that the church be not split on racial grounds. Gal. 2.

Paul's praise of the uncultured classes. I Cor. 1: 18–2: 5.

Paul's fundamental principles that no artificial strata of society can
be admitted by the church. Gal. 3: 23–29; Col. 3: 5–11.

Paul's teaching of the unity of the church. Eph. 4: 1–16.

When we realize that it was as hard in the days of the apostles for
Jew and Greek to sit down and eat together as it is for white and
black in America today, that it was as hard for men to admit their
oneness of humanity with women as in any male ascendancy of the
twentieth century, we shall understand how realistically and how
courageously the apostles wrought the Christian faith.

CHRISTIAN EXPERIENCE AND THE CALENDAR

The varying points of emphasis in Christian experience are
governed by the calendar to a greater degree than most of us realize.
While we would not artificially limit reading to the seasons, or line
up just those passages of the Bible that are suitable at certain times
of the year, nevertheless we do well to take advantage of the pause
in life given by the recurrence of well-remembered dates.

Family Anniversaries

There are the occasions, dear to every household, of wedding
anniversaries, birthdays, or some significant happenings. At such
times it will be especially fitting to read notable passages of the
Bible that stress family relationships or that call to courage in facing
the future.

The family is such a recurrent theme that its influence is to be felt in parts of the Bible too numerous to mention. Some of the special passages that might be emphasized are these:

The family as the unit for religious instruction, Deut. 6.
Hannah's passion for a family, I Sam. 1–3.
Proverbs of the family, Prov., 1–9, 31, and many single verses.
The prophet's use of the family figure, Hos. 11.
Jesus and his family, using the references given above under that head.
Jesus' teaching on the family, Mark 10: 1–16.
Jesus and God's Fatherhood, Luke 15.
Paul and the family, Eph. 5: 15–6: 9.

National Anniversaries

The Bible throws strong emphasis on the state. This is especially true of the Old Testament where church and state are one. In these days when so much new attention is being given to forms of government and to national and international affairs, it will be well to guard our national anniversaries against sentimentality by linking them strongly with religion.

On Independence Day we may well read the story of Israel winning its independence from Egypt, with its emphasis on divine aid and even divine intervention. The best part of the story is in Exodus, chapters 12–15. Or we may read some story of deliverance of the days of the judges, such as that under Deborah and Barak, Judges chapters 4, 5. Such Psalms as the 124th and 126th breathe fervently the spirit of release from oppression. They even suggest the spiritualizing of freedom which the Christian should always look to on Independence Day, freedom from the greatest of all oppressors, sin. For this emphasis the great passages are John, chapter 8, and Romans, chapter 8. These two chapters merit much rereading.

Other days, such as Memorial Day, are apt to be celebrated merely by parades of uniforms. The Christian can do much to turn the emphasis to peace. He should read, not only privately, but publicly, wherever possible on these days, such passages as the prophetic vision of peace, Isa. 2: 1–4; Micah 4: 1–5, and the prediction of the

Prince of Peace, Isa. 9: 1-7. He should read many of the passages listed under experiences of human relations, for it is the good will resulting from noble actions of man toward man that is needed to make peace. "If possible . . . live peaceably with all" (Rom. 12: 18). Of course, the angels' song of good will comes to mind, Luke 2: 8-14, and once again the Christian will spiritualize such passages by remembering that inner peace which the world cannot give, but which it cannot take away even in time of bloody strife. For this, the comforting 14th chapter of John is our priceless possession. It seems almost a homily on the lovely saying of Isa. 26: 3.

Thanksgiving Day most frequently of our national anniversaries has been associated with religious thought. The Psalms listed in chapter 7 as Psalms of Thanksgiving are all suggestive for this occasion, but to these should be added from the Old Testament the law of the thank offering, Lev. 7: 11-18, and Habakkuk's glorious Psalm of thanksgiving for God in the midst of invasion, Hab., chapter 3. In the New Testament the example of Jesus at the feeding of the multitude is important, John 6: 1-13, with which compare Paul's comment in I Cor. 11: 23. The case of the thankful leper is unforgettable, Luke 17: 11-19. Paul's letters are full of the spirit of thankfulness, especially such of the shorter ones as Ephesians, Colossians, Philippians, I and II Thessalonians. The reading of any one of these letters on Thanksgiving Day will be rewarding. And the central section of II Corinthians, chapters 8, 9, is a splendid commentary on the giving of gifts as an expression of thankfulness for God's greatest gift.

Vacation Time

The carefree spirit suggested by these national holidays reminds us of the fact that too many Christians make a holiday from their religion out of a vacation trip. Real joy awaits the one who will prepare his schedule for his Bible reading during the vacation as carefully as he marks his road maps or packs his bags. Not that there is much in the Bible bearing on an outing, but that the vacation time is a peculiarly fitting season for sharing the frequent experience of biblical authors with God's great out-of-doors.

There is that large group of Psalms that have in them so much rejoicing in nature, and such apt use of figures from nature, such as numbers 1, 8, 18, 19, 23, 29, 33, 36, 42–43, 46, 57, 65, 72, 76, 77, 80, 84, 90, 91, 93, 96, 97, 98, 104, 105, 107, 113, 114, 121, 124, 126, 136, 139, 144, 147, 148. All of these make good reading out in the open, the special favorites being numbers 8, 19, 46, 84, 93, 104, 121, and 148. Then there are many great messages of the prophets that are based on figures from nature. Of special note are the prophecies of Amos, Micah's gigantic figure of the mountain court in the sixth chapter of his book, Isaiah's wonderful use of nature in such chapters as the fifth, the fortieth, and the fifty-fifth, and Jeremiah's pictures of shepherds and fig orchards, chapters 23 and 24. The Sinai and Nebo experiences of Moses, Exodus 19, Deuteronomy 32–34, are more suggestive when read at least on a hilltop, while Elijah's contrasting mountains of Carmel and the wilderness, as told in I Kings 18 and 19, beckon the spirit to the heights. The mind of the Master is understood with greater clarity when we read far from the haunts of men such gospel passages as those of his desert temptation, Matt. 4: 1–11, or his "Sermon on the Mount," Matt., chapters 5–7, or his transfiguration, Mark 9: 1–13, his teaching by the lakeside and his calming of the storm on that lake as told in Mark 4, his feeding of the multitude and subsequent walking on the waves as pictured in John 6, and especially his final surrender of himself to his Father in the thick of the garden, Mark 14: 32–42.

The Church Calendar

Several of the more ritualistic Protestant groups follow the custom of the Roman and Greek churches and of the Jews in assigning certain passages of Scripture to be read publicly, the calendar of readings being made out for every week of the year. While no church goes so far as to require certain passages to be read privately at these times, almost all of us are accustomed to emphasizing particular thoughts in our reading at appropriate seasons in the church's activity. Thus some clarion call to new endeavor, such as that of Joshua 1, is often used in the fall when renewed activities begin in most congregations. But it is around the Christmas and the Easter seasons that we witness the larger part of what we may call "occasional reading" of the Bible.

Now it is a mistake to limit Christmas reading to the birth stories of Matthew 1, 2, and Luke 1, 2. This is a good time to gather together those prophetic references to Messiah that the Christian, in the light of his New Testament, has long seen fulfilled in Jesus. The best of these are:

The first promise of redemption, Gen. 3, esp. vv. 14, 15.
The blessing of the tribe of Judah, Gen. 49: 8–12.
Moses' vision of the Prophet, Deut. 18: 15–19.
God's promise to the house of David, II Sam. 7.
The Messianic Psalms, as listed in chapter 7.
The peace passages, Micah 4: 1–5, Isa. 2: 1–4; 9: 1–7.
The Servant passages, Isa. 42: 1–9; 43: 1–7; 44: 1–5; 49: 1–7; 52: 13–
  53: 12.
The prophecy of Bethlehem, Micah 5: 2–4.
The Lord's messenger, Malachi 3: 1–6.

Similarly, during the weeks preceding Easter, it is not enough to read again the passion narrative from the last chapters of the four Gospels. This should never be neglected. It may be read one year from one Gospel, the next from another, and so on, or it may be read as one story from the harmony arrangement of passages outlined in chapter 8. But this is also the most appropriate time to reread some of the great passages on the "Suffering Servant" listed above from Isaiah. Jesus himself used these passages in application to himself more than he used the Messianic Psalms. Especially fitting are Isa. 42: 1–9; 49: 1–13; chapters 52, 53; and the paragraph which Jesus later used in the Nazareth synagogue as the basis for his ministry, Isa. 61: 1–3, as used in Luke 4: 16–21. Perhaps the lenten season may be rendered most impressive by reading these passages from Isaiah first, then the narrative of Jesus' last week from the Gospels, and finally the story of the resurrection from the four. The Eastertide should be climaxed with other portions of the New Testament, reading I Cor. 15, the great apostolic discussion of men's resurrection, Paul's spiritual interpretation of resurrection in Romans 6, Jesus' own spiritual interpretation in John 11 at the raising of Lazarus, and finally the vision of the renewed world in Revelation 21, 22. For all the apostles and preachers of the church have emphasized the fact that the resurrection is the cornerstone of the gospel, and that Easter means to us all the power of life in God.

Chapter 10

READING THE BIBLE WITH CHILDREN

The Bible is a family book. The experiences of life described in the last chapter are, for the most part, family experiences. From the earliest times the Hebrew-Christian tradition, represented in our Old and New Testaments, was intended to be communicated to rising generations in family situations: "And these words which I command you this day shall be upon your heart; and you shall teach them diligently to your children, and shall talk of them when you sit in your house, and when you walk by the way, and when you lie down, and when you rise" (Deut. 6: 6, 7).

Nevertheless, the Bible is written to adults. Its language and point of view are adult. Its purpose is to persuade and ground those who are able to think and reason. Its writers nowhere attempt to adapt their thought to the child mind. They leave that entirely to the heads of the families that make up the believing households. Education in things religious has been the age-long custom both of Hebrews and of Christians, but the Bible itself was not written as a book of religious education for children.

It is, of course, possible to read the Bible to the very young, or even to put it into their own hands. John Ruskin's mother is said to have required him to read the Bible through when he was three years of age, poring over its difficult passages and spelling out its hard words. Ruskin testifies to this early experience as the source of his wonderful literary style. But probably most of us would prefer to take a little less in the way of style and not run the risk of turning our children against the very book we want them to learn to love by forcing its reading upon them as a chore. If they are to read or to have read to them the text of the King James or any other English Bible, some idea is needed of how to proceed in choosing the best passages.

Principles of Selection

It will readily occur to most parents to follow up the usual procedure of the Sunday school and the Vacation Bible School by selecting for their children's reading those parts of the Bible that tell stories about children. Once more, it must be borne in mind that these stories are not written from the child's point of view, and if read in the Bible text itself, some of them may not prove interesting to young children. But there is at least a meeting point if a child is the center of the story. Such Old Testament passages as those of the youthful Isaac and his father, the early part of the stories of Joseph and Samuel, the boy-king Joash, the Shunammite boy raised to life by Elisha, and such New Testament stories as those of Jesus' childhood, Jesus' love for children, his bringing life to the little girl in the ruler's home, and the feeding of the multitude, with the ever appealing little boy's lunch, come readily to mind. The number of such incidents is limited, though children of course like to hear the same story over and over again.

In the case of the Old Testament, stories with family group settings may be read to quite young children, if the parent will make wise omissions of the parts that deal with experiences beyond their grasp. Thus the family lives of Abraham and Isaac, of Jacob and Joseph, of Moses and Jephthah and Ruth, and of David as part of the family of Saul, may be handled.

Most of the passages suggested in the last chapter as dealing with great experiences of life make good family reading. Thus, under the heading "Great Experiences with God," practically everything can be used effectively with children except the passages from Hosea and Habakkuk. Not that they will understand all that is being read, but that these passages carry enough of the elemental expression of awe and wonder to live in the child's memory in a wholesome way. Under the heading "Notable Relationships Between People," the passages suggested (again with the exception of Hosea) are fine for stressing principles of right and wrong, truth and falsehood, kindness and brutality, since these are most readily grasped in scenes of vivid contrast. The latter part of this section, "The Wider Relations," contains passages that will seem to many parents too old for children under eleven or twelve. The latter part of the chapter, "Christian Experience and the Calendar," is again very useful, as most of the passages suggested here have natural family affinities.

Many parents ask the question, "Should children be encouraged to read the blood-and-thunder stories of the historical books of the Old Testament?" Perhaps the best answer is that it depends on the story. The idea that the child will be horrified by such tales is all very nice, but it lacks reality. Children do not necessarily recoil from stories of plunder and killing and conquest. Witness their reaction to the detective programs of the television show or the murder scenes of the movies. Yet many parents seek earnestly to protect their children against such tales, especially where there is no moral or where the moral is not obvious. Scarcely any tale of the Bible will harrow the nerves of a child, but there are Old Testament stories of terror where the moral is elemental and on the surface, while there are other stories where the moral is by no means apparent and may even tax adult experience to appreciate it. Thus in the tale of the drowning of the Egyptians in the Red Sea, the background of the character and attitude of Pharaoh makes the moral effect easy to grasp and good to experience, but most children will be less likely to see the ethical in the bloody stories of Samson and the Philistines, while the solemn sense of duty that prompts Samuel to "hew Agag to pieces before the Lord" (I Sam. 15: 33) is entirely adult. Even in the book of Acts in the New Testament, children will vary in their appreciation of the reason for many of the violent judgments that proceed from the Holy Spirit. (See especially, Acts, ch. 5.) In general, we need to emphasize with children those parts of the Bible where basic principles of morals are readily seen.

It is a common belief that the Old Testament rather than the New is the children's book. This belief needs changing. While it is true that there are more books in the Old Testament which contain material in story form, the Gospels ought to be the child's chief reading from the Bible. Over and over again the stories of the life of Jesus should be read, sometimes as single events, and sometimes in one Gospel read straight through.

It is wise to note that the Gospels differ in their appeal to children, and, for that matter, to all age groups. In general, the Gospel of Mark is the children's Gospel, because of its stress on activity and its vivid portrayals. The Gospel of Luke is especially good for the early and middle teens, because then its idealizations are most apt to be appreciated. Older young people often like the tone of argument in the Gospel of John. Matthew is the most adult of all the Gospels, because of its sermonizing. But when all this is said, we should remember that we are dealing in generalizations; for the beatitudes in Matthew, for example, should be among the child's earliest memorization of more than a single verse. The Gospel of John comes more nearly to abstract thought than do any of the first three, and therefore will probably appeal less to children in spite of its being the best beloved of the four by many of the fathers and mothers.

Unit Readings of the Bible for Children

Is it possible now to take the principles discussed above and with them select passages from the Bible that will give assured results in reading with children? Not if we should try to grade them according to the various age groups under twelve. Indeed, any application of our principles of reading the actual text of the Bible to children will vary greatly with individuals and with family situations. Any suggestions that one may make can be readily criticized at this point or that, but for the sake of being as helpful as we may in following out the line already undertaken, the following table is offered as containing most of the passages that will be found to be especially useful with children somewhere between the ages of six and twelve. The units of reading referred to are those outlined in chapters 7 and 8.

Genesis, because it deals with men in relation to God and to each other. By looking ahead, parents will readily sense parts of chapters that should be omitted.

Exodus, units 1–3 (chapters 1–20) and unit 6 (chapters 32–34) because they deal with the stories of Moses and two accounts of the giving of the commandments.

Leviticus, not at all, because it deals with ritual law which is entirely uninteresting to children.

Numbers, units 2, a and b (chapters 10–14), and 3, a (chapters 22–24), because they deal with interesting stories of events. The remainder of the book of Numbers is concerned either with more ritual law or with events of judgment requiring interpretation.

Deuteronomy, except for the lengthy unit 2, b (chapters 12–26), where the detail of law may become wearisome to children. Children should get good impressions from the other parts of the book, especially from unit 3, "The blessing and the curse" (chapters 27–30).

Joshua, units 1, a and b (chapters 1–9), because of their interesting narratives of conquest, and unit 3 (chapters 23–24) because of Joshua's noble address. Other parts of the book consist of details of conquest that have little interest for children.

Judges, units 1–5 (chapters 1–16), because of their vivid narrative, though some of the stories may leave the wrong ethical impression on the child unless the parent is careful to talk over their significance. The last five chapters of the book of Judges are too obscure to read to children.

Ruth, entire, as a story.

I Samuel, units 1, a (chapters 1–3), 2, a (chapters 9–12), and 3 (chapters 16–31), because of their interesting stories of the early life of three outstanding heroes.

II Samuel, units 1–3 (chapters 1–10), because they deal with the good side of David, and unit 6 (chapters 15–20) because of its fascinating recital of the story of Absalom's revolt. There are poetic passages in unit 7 (chapters 21–24) which give worthy descriptions of the closing years of David.

I Kings, unit 1, a and b (chapters 1–4), and unit 3, a (chapters 17–19), should surely be read to children because of their dealing respectively with the life stories of Solomon and Elijah. Perhaps the other sections of I Kings are, for most children, too involved in the intricacies of Hebrew history to be appreciated.

II Kings, unit 1 (chapters 1–8); the stories of Elisha make fine reading for children. Possibly unit 2 (chapters 9–11), because of the good priest and the boy king. Certainly unit 4 (chapters 18–20), the story of Hezekiah's faith. Possibly units 5 and 6 (chapters 21–25) for the historical interest in the fall of the Hebrew kingdom.

I and II Chronicles are somewhat more meditative and lack the movement of the books of Kings. Since they are so largely repetitious of Kings anyway, they need not be repeated with children.

Ezra, unit 1 (chapters 1–6, omitting chapter 2), because of its description of the rebuilding of the temple. The remainder of Ezra has to do with his work of purification.

Nehemiah, units 1 and 2 (chapters 1–7, omitting chapters 3 and 7), because of their stories of the rebuilding of the walls of Jerusalem. The remainder of Nehemiah, like Ezra, is concerned mostly with ritualistic purification.

Esther, entire, as a story.

Job is difficult to deal with in reading to children. The first two chapters and the last make an interesting story, and if they can be tied together without reading too much of the argument that comes in between, they will awaken interest.

Psalms. The best Psalms to read to children are those of classes 1–3, 5–8, 15 and 16, of the groupings given in chapter 7.

Proverbs is best handled with children by reading a few at a time every now and then. The number scheme of chapter 30 interests some children.

Ecclesiastes and the Song of Solomon do not offer material for children's reading.

The Prophets. It is desirable to introduce children early to the Prophets of the Old Testament, especially to stories of their lives and to beautiful expressions of their preaching. It is hard to interest children, however, in reading much from the Prophets.

Isaiah has many passages of sheer beauty that quicken the sense of awe. The best chapters are 6, 9, 35, 40, 41, 52, 53, 55, 58, 60, and 61.

Jeremiah, chapter 1, for the Prophet's call.

Chapters 18 and 19, the stories of the potter.

Chapter 31, the New Covenant, to which may be added chapters 32 and 33.

Chapter 35, a story of obedience.

Chapter 36, the burning of Jeremiah's writing.

Chapters 37–39, Jeremiah and the fall of Jerusalem, a passage which may well be read with the last selection from II Kings.

Lamentations is not a children's book.

Many of Ezekiel's figures are too involved and too obscure for use with children. Chapter 33, the story of the watchman, will best represent this Prophet for them. With some older children certain of Ezekiel's parables may be added, especially his vision of the valley of dry bones (chapter 37).

Daniel, all of unit 1 (chapters 1–6). The remainder of Daniel is again too obscure for the child who is unacquainted with ancient history.

Hosea, in spite of its great beauty and worth, offers little that will appeal to children, except possibly chapter 11.

Joel contains vivid imagery and appeals to the imagination, but is too difficult to explain to children.

Amos is again above them in spite of many fine separate sayings in unit 2 (chapters 3–6).

Obadiah has nothing special for children.

Jonah should be read entire as a story.

Micah, units 3 and 4 (chapters 4–7), will probably be attractive to some children.

The remainder of the Minor Prophets should be left for later years, except for the book of Haggai, which may be read as the prophetic story of the rebuilding of the temple.

The Gospels have already been discussed in their peculiar applicabilities.

Matthew, Mark, and Luke should be read in their entirety. Probably John also, in spite of its tendency to abstract thought.

Acts, entire, as the history of the early church and its experiences, though parts of it will be obscure to children.

Romans is too logical in its thought for the child mind, but chapter 8 should be read for its sheer magnificence, and chapter 12 for its practical injunctions.

I Corinthians deals with church problems in a way that can hardly interest children. Unit 3, a (chapters 8–10) may make an interesting story for some of them. Certainly chapters 13 and 15 should be read.

II Corinthians will be best represented by unit 2 (chapters 8 and 9), where the apostle's ideals of giving may be grasped.

The remainder of the Pauline Letters offers little of direct value to
   children, except Ephesians, chapter 6, and the little letter to
   Philemon, if its story element can be caught.
Hebrews will be best represented by chapters 11 and 13.
James, like Proverbs, can perhaps best be read to children a bit at a
   time, but it should all prove attractive.
The Letters of Peter are not inviting to children.
The Letters of John may be omitted, unless II John, written to a lady
   and her children, may evoke some interest.
Jude also may be passed by.
The Book of Revelation can best be represented by units 1 (chapters
   1–3) and 9 (chapters 21 and 22).

Using Various Versions

So far we have been proceeding on the assumption that most
people who read the Bible to their children will use the King James
Version. Its years of popularity have been richly deserved. Its beauty
and ruggedness of speech have woven their way into the very warp
and woof of our language, so that our commonest expressions come
from it. Its sonorousness of sound has been the adoration of three
centuries. Yet it is possible to be too poetic in expression and not
poetic enough in the form which the writing takes on the page.

From the standpoint of interesting children in the Bible (and
adults too for that matter), the Revised Standard Version has
several real advantages. For one thing it prints the poetry of the
Bible in poetic form, not only in the Book of Psalms, but in the
prophets and in much of the New Testament. For another, it groups
its sentences into paragraphs after the fashion of other books. This
is especially important as a help to children who are old enough to
read the Bible themselves, for the paragraph is the most natural unit
of thought. And again the Revision makes use of quotation marks,
so that in dialogue one is aided in knowing just who is speaking.

Many parents have also found that by introducing their children
to some of the modern speech versions they give them the thrill of
a new discovery. The translations of Weymouth and of Moffatt
have appealed to a goodly number. Goodspeed's New Testament

and, later, the entire Smith and Goodspeed Bible, known as "The American Translation," have proved quite attractive and are certainly clear and idiomatic in their translation of the Gospels in particular. More lately the Phillips translations have commended themselves to many, especially to young people. It must be remembered that all these are free versions. They do not attempt, as does the Revised Standard Version, to be exact as translations, but rather to make readable and vivid the sense of the passages as they render them into the best English of our day.

BOOKS OF BIBLE STORIES

While the text of the Bible itself in one or more of the versions noted above may be used with children, it is the present writer's feeling that at least up to the age of eight, it is better to employ series of Bible stories, especially those that are well illustrated.

For children who are just beginning to read, we are fortunate in having such stories which look very much like their school primers, having a few large words on each page with a picture opposite. Children soon learn to love the reading of these little books. As they get somewhat older, they will find most inviting too, books which tell in a simple, straightforward way, and with good use of imagination, the stories of Bible heroes and Bible ideas. The best of all these types of books are noted in the Bibliography with comments on each. We still need someone to write the stories of the Old Testament prophets and of the New Testament letters in a form suitable for children. There are, however, in the church school courses of some of our denominations, excellent presentations of the Bible in continued story form. In some of the best of these, Bible story books that are so bound as to be permanent parts of the child's library are of inestimable aid. They invite the parent to read with the children.

One of the most valuable practices in reading the Bible with children or in general family situations is the use of the hymnbook along with the Word of God. Whether or not you have a musical instrument in your home, invest in two or three good hymnals (not cheap songbooks), and use the topical index frequently along with your Bibles. You may read a portion of a Bible story to the children and with it a hymn that was suggested by it or is related to it. Thus with the ever interesting account of Jacob's vision at Bethel, the great hymn "Nearer, My God, to Thee" may well be read or sung in its entirety, for most of its stanzas are direct reflections of this story. "We Are Climbing Jacob's Ladder" is of course also closely related to the same influential narrative. Or there is in the Gospel of Mark the tale of Jesus healing the crowds that gathered around Peter's home in the evening (Mark 1: 32–34). From its suggestive picture was born the beautiful hymn "At even when the sun did set, The sick, O Lord, around Thee lay." The alert parent, with the use of the hymnal index and perhaps a good book on hymns, will easily multiply these illustrations rapidly. The double impression left by scripture and hymn is among the most lasting for youth. A child who early learns to sing his religion is apt to grow most fruitfully in his faith.

Chapter 11

KINDS OF LITERATURE IN THE BIBLE

This book is not a commentary on the Bible. Its purpose is to suggest ways of reading the Bible, not how to interpret it. Nevertheless reading and interpretation are closely related. "Do you understand what you are reading?" may well be asked one Christian by another as Philip asked the Ethiopian eunuch (Acts 8: 30). One of the first tools in interpreting is the understanding of the kind of literature one is reading. It is hardly possible to make sense if one is not aware whether the material read is prose or poetry, truth or fiction, drama or sober fact.

INTERMINGLING OF LITERARY FORMS

One of the most surprising discoveries about the Bible is the way in which its style can pass from one literary form to another and mingle in the same passage two or more kinds of literature. We are accustomed to thinking of prose and poetry as quite distinct. But in the Bible they are mixed freely, and are almost merged in places, especially in the prophets. The reason is largely this: the meaning that poetry has for the authors of the Bible is quite different from its meaning to us. True enough, much is being published as poetry today that seems nothing more than prose arranged in lines of various lengths. Still, we think of poetry as usually having rhyme, and almost always having meter. Our classical poetry can all be lined off, so many feet to the verse.

Biblical Poetry

But in the Bible these distinctions of poetry are not found. There is seldom any rhyme or formal meter. Even the rhythm is of different nature than ours. The poetry of the Bible depends on what we call "parallelism," that is, the balance of one line against another in length or in thought or both. This is essentially a Hebrew style, and the large part of the poetry of the Bible is found, of course, in the Old Testament. But in the New Testament too the Hebrew forms are used even in the Greek language, and the same recurring balance of one thought against another, of one line with a second, is to be noted. Very frequently the second line is but the repetition of the idea in the first, phrased a little differently or with synonyms used for the principal words. This accounts for the large amount of repetition of words, phrases, and ideas in the Bible. In reading the Bible people sometimes laboriously try to get different meanings out of parallel thoughts when none are intended. Thus in the shortest Psalm, the 117th:

> Praise the Lord, all nations!
>   Extol him, all peoples!
> For great is his steadfast love toward us;
>   and the faithfulness of the Lord
>   endures forever.
> Praise the Lord!

No distinction is intended between "nations" and "peoples." The Psalmist's poetic feeling is satisfied by issuing his call to praise twice, addressing his audience once as "nations" and the next time as "peoples." Thus the first two lines are in parallelism. Similarly with the third and fourth lines. "His steadfast love toward us" and "The faithfulness of the Lord" mean essentially the same thing. The final "Praise the Lord" is, of course, simply our translation of the Hebrew "Hallelujah."

Unfortunately, in our King James English Bible, these balanced clauses are not printed as separate lines of poetry. The reader will often find them surprisingly easy to recognize, though being able to see them on the printed page helps a great deal. Since the Revised Standard Version has printed in poetic form not only the Psalms but also much of the prophets and other portions of the scriptures, the sense is greatly aided by following its arrangements. Thus in the glorious fifty-fifth chapter of Isaiah the same delight in the balanced lines appears quite clearly when we see those lines set off in metrical couplets or stanzas:

> Seek the Lord while he may be found,
>   call upon him while he is near;
> let the wicked forsake his way,
>   and the unrighteous man his thoughts;
> let him return to the Lord, that he may have mercy on him,
>   and to our God, for he will abundantly pardon.

Here it is easy to see that the first and second lines balance each other in thought and length, and mean essentially the same thing. The same is true of the third and fourth, and also of the fifth and sixth. The slight variations in the wording make the repeated invitation to resound with beautiful cadences.

As in any language, poetry is the utterance of the imagination. The biblical writer uses poetic license as any other writer does. He does not mean literally the personification of natural objects, as, for instance, in the twelfth verse of the same fifty-fifth chapter of Isaiah:

> For you shall go out in joy,
>   and be led forth in peace;
> the mountains and the hills before you
>   shall break forth into singing,
>   and all the trees of the field shall clap their hands.

No one would imagine that even in the Bible the writer meant that mountains and hills would sing songs or that trees had actual hands they would clap. It is not even necessary to suppose that the poet thought of the branches of the trees as their hands. What would be the voices of the hills? But he is poetically reveling in the delight of nature at the onward march of God's people. In such a case this is easily recognized. Yet there are many other passages in the Bible, often taken literally, which, when studied in the light of these balanced lines, are just as truly poetry. For example, the oft-quoted passage from the twenty-sixth chapter of Isaiah,

> Thy dead shall live, their bodies shall rise.

This is sometimes used as an Old Testament proof of the resurrection of the body. But read in its highly poetic setting the expression "Thy dead" is seen to mean those that are spiritually dead, and since the second half of the line is poetic parallelism, the words "their bodies" mean simply the same as "Thy dead." The New Testament does indeed give us, both in prose and in poetry, many accounts of the actual resurrection of the body. But there is no object in reading back into this passage from Isaiah a thought that we as Christians revel in, simply to try to find some early corroboration for it. Much will be gained for sensible Bible reading when we learn not to try to make a passage mean something that some similarly sounding verse does mean just in order to have added proof. We can afford to take versification for its own sake.

The chief kind of poetry in the Bible is lyric. In fact this predominates so greatly as to leave all others far behind. A lyric is a poetic expression of a personal experience, and the frequency of lyric in the Bible makes it clear that the best way to further the knowledge and love of God is to give utterance to that which one knows firsthand—his own experience with God. As a matter of fact this is all one really does know in any way of which he can bear witness. Lyric is thus essentially religious. Consider, for example, how the twenty-third Psalm would sound if it read like this:

> The Lord is a shepherd, man shall not want.

Here is a perfectly true statement, and in the same rhythm, but it loses much of its appeal. The twenty-third Psalm has sung its way into human hearts everywhere just because its writer sang it originally out of the depths of his own heart's knowledge of God:

> The Lord is my shepherd, I shall not want.

There are forms of poetry in the Bible which defy classification as simple lyrics, yet even in the serious and philosophically minded odes, and in the elaborate anthems, the lyric element is still present. Thus the triumph song of Deborah over the fall of Sisera, as it is preserved in Judges 5, is a fine ode to the occasion, yet its alternating shouts of triumph and of curse breathe the bitterness and the fierce joy of very personal experiences. Thus individual experience and group sharing are often mingled in the religious poem. Such a national anthem as the 105th Psalm can affirm in personal reflection,

> He is the Lord our God;
> his judgments are in all the earth.

Biblical writers love to dramatize. The prophets staged not only many of their actions, but much of their speech. There are presentations of nature, such as the ninety-third Psalm or the twenty-ninth Psalm, or the latter part of the fifty-fifth chapter of Isaiah, that are rich in histrionic art. The book of Job is frequently thought of as a religious drama to be acted out on the stage, with the "Dramatis Personae" well defined.

Biblical writers also loved the idea of epic, though most of the biblical epic is in prose rather than in poetry. Thus the stories of the patriarchs in the book of Genesis are really epic cycles of their wanderings. By some the book of Job is regarded as the epic of a soul, groping its way through the experiences of earth to its God.

It should always be borne in mind that when we speak of a book or a passage of the Bible as being drama or epic, we do not mean that it is untrue historically. It may be straight history, or it may be founded upon history, or it may be the creation of the imagination for the purpose of teaching a religious lesson. In all events the drama or the epic is true in the highest sense. To say that the book of Job, for example, is "the epic of the inner life," as one writer calls it, is not to say that the story never happened. It may all have occurred in every detail to some actual individual by the name of Job, and have been cast in epic or dramatic form by some great religious writer. Or it may be based roughly on some known experience. Or it may be fictional as far as any one character is concerned, but true to life in that it represents the road traveled by many souls before they are completely found by God.

BIBLICAL HISTORY

We have already noted in our consideration of Samuel, Kings, and Chronicles, in chapters 6 and 7, that history as mere impassive narrative does not occur in the Bible. If there is such a thing as an unbiased account of events, a scientifically accurate history, the Bible is not interested in it. And we may well be glad that this is so. There is no religion in mere facts. Facts always need interpretation. They need the reaction of minds that have played over them. This is abundantly true of what we call the historical books of our Bible, in both Old and New Testaments. The writers of the history of Israel, of the life of Christ, of the story of the early church, all believed in facts. The religion they have passed on to us is founded on facts. But they have always gone on to give us their interpretation of the facts. As we have observed before, the books of the Kings tell the story of the fortunes of the Hebrew kingdom as the prophets of the day saw them, while the books of the Chronicles tell the same story as the priests of a later day saw it. In a similiar way Matthew, Mark, Luke, and John are "historical," as we would say, but they are *Gospels*, that is, they are a good-news interpretation of the history of Jesus. The book of the Acts is a history of the spread of the early church, seen through the eyes of a traveling companion of Paul by the name of Luke. No history in the Bible is unbiased. It is all written to show something, to convert the mind and heart to the religious point of view which makes the Bible so much more than history. For when a writer is reliable, his having a purpose in mind is not only no hindrance, it is a tremendous help.

The effect of this truth upon the structure of the Old Testament is especially noteworthy. All the writers among the Jews, whether prophets or priests, considered their people peculiarly chosen by God, heirs of the covenant. Their historical books may be called "the history of the holy," using the word "holy" in its original sense of "set apart." This effect is most clearly seen in the fact that the Jews did not class any of the books of their Bible as history. Exodus, for example, comes under the "law." Kings comes under the "prophets," because written from the prophets' point of view. Chronicles, on the other hand, is classified with the "sacred writings," where all the poetical and priestly collections are to be found. A comparative table of the Jews' arrangement of the Old Testament and of ours will make clear this idea of "history."

Arrangement of Books

Our Old Testament	The Jewish Old Testament
I. The five books of Moses	I. The Law
1. Genesis	1. Genesis
2. Exodus	2. Exodus
3. Leviticus	3. Leviticus
4. Numbers	4. Numbers
5. Deuteronomy	5. Deuteronomy
II. The historical books	II. The Prophets
6. Joshua	a. The former prophets
7. Judges	6. Joshua
8. Ruth	7. Judges
9. I Samuel	8. Samuel
10. II Samuel	9. Kings
11. I Kings	b. The latter prophets
12. II Kings	10. Isaiah
13. I Chronicles	11. Jeremiah
14. II Chronicles	12. Ezekiel
15. Ezra	13. The book of the twelve
16. Nehemiah	(containing our twelve "minor prophets" counted as one book)
17. Esther	
III. The poetical books	III. The Sacred Writings
18. Job	a. The three books (using "book" in our sense of a volume)
19. Psalms	14. Psalms
20. Proverbs	15. Proverbs
21. Ecclesiastes	16. Job
22. Song of Solomon	

Our Old Testament, cont.

IV. The prophets
  a. The major prophets
    23. Isaiah
    24. Jeremiah, with
    25. Lamentations of Jeremiah
    26. Ezekiel
    27. Daniel
  b. The minor prophets
    28. Hosea
    29. Joel
    30. Amos
    31. Obadiah
    32. Jonah
    33. Micah
    34. Nahum
    35. Habakkuk
    36. Zephaniah
    37. Haggai
    38. Zechariah
    39. Malachi

Jewish Old Testament, cont.

  b. The rolls or scrolls (so called because the writings were short enough to get each on one temple roll)
    17. Ruth
    18. Esther
    19. Song of Songs
    20. Ecclesiastes
    21. Lamentations
  c. The "others"
    22. Daniel
    23. Ezra-Nehemiah (considered as one book)
    24. Chronicles

From the above list it will be observed that exactly the same books occur in the Jewish Old Testament as in ours, but the arrangement is quite different. We get 39 by our grouping, while they get but 24. We have a fairly large class of "historical books"; they recognize no such class. They put some of our historical books under the prophets, others under the temple scrolls, and Chronicles is placed with the "writings." Nor is this simply in the interest of emphasizing the prophets with as long a list as possible, for the book of Daniel, which we classify with the prophets, is not considered a book of prophecy in the Hebrew Old Testament. The reason for this will be observed in its place. The point here is that so strong is the conviction that history is written from particular points of view that all the books which we call historical are placed by the Jews in the classes which represent their several viewpoints.

BIBLICAL PROPHECY

But what do we mean by saying that books of history are written from the point of view of prophets? Is not a prophet one who fore-tells the future, and does not history deal with the past?

Nothing could more clearly show the conception which the ancient Hebrews had of their prophets than this classification of history with the prophetic writings. For the idea of a prophet is not primarily one who *fore*-tells, but one who *forth*-tells. The word "prophet" comes from a verb meaning "to speak for." It is the verb of the messenger, one who utters a word for another. The prophet did indeed have predictions to make about the future, whether in terms of particular events or of principles according to which results might be expected. But the prophet was primarily a preacher, a proclaimer of the word of God to his own day, with the purpose of changing the lives of the people of that day. So he wrote history in such a way as to show why the people had suffered and why they had prospered. He described his visions in such a way as to display God's knowledge of the nation's inner life. The prophets spoke to the worshipers, the politicians, the traders, the social classes of their day. It is a mistake to use the books of the prophets as stamping grounds for finding the predictions of this or that particular happening centuries in advance. So to use them is to close the mind to their original purpose. The prophets' predictions grew out of their sermons of evangelistic fervor, as hope must ever emerge from warning if the preacher knows his God.

BIBLICAL APOCALYPTIC

This leads to the noting of a kind of literature close akin to prophecy yet quite distinct from it. The word "apocalypse" is not so familiar to the average English reader as the words "prophecy," "history," and "lyric." Yet it denotes just as definite a form of literature as any of the others.

"Apocalypse" means literally "a taking off of the veil." It is the same word in the Greek that "revelation" is in the Latin. But apocalyptic literature was written in times of persecution when it was unsafe to say in plain language what was meant. It was intended to veil the thought from those who were uninitiated. It was intended to "take off the veil" for those who could understand. For apocalyptic literature was definitely written in code. It succeeded to the literary throne, so to speak, as prophecy waned, and it continued to use many of the methods of the prophetic type of literature. It was sermonic like prophecy; it dealt in visions and in explanations of the word of the Lord and in predictions of the future. Like prophecy it was concerned with the conditions of the times, but it emphasized far more than the prophet had done the evil of the times, the immediacy of impending judgment, and especially the catastrophic nature of any change that must take place before peace and good should reign. Thus the apocalyptist became pessimistic about the troublous days in which he lived. He believed the powers that ruled his day were evil. He encouraged his people to expect their overthrow. He placed little hope in progress or growth, but felt that all anticipation of righteousness was bound up in destruction of the powers of sin. He emphasized the future rather than the present of the kingdom of God.

It is probably this stress on the evil nature of the present that accounts for the custom of the apocalyptist using a secret code. These present powers of evil were usually in the ascendancy. To speak out against them might mean uselessly throwing one's life away. Yet the righteous must be encouraged to hope, and so the hidden message to them.

The amount of apocalyptic literature in the Bible is surprising. Traces of it occur in Isaiah. Ezekiel has quite a bit of it. The second half of Zechariah is an apocalypse. The great example in the Old Testament is the book of Daniel. If the prevalence of this type ended with the Old Testament, we should not be nearly so much concerned with it. But the New Testament is full of it too. Jesus' discourse on "last things," as we called it in the reading units for the Gospels, employs the apocalyptic style and imagery throughout.

Paul uses it, especially in his letters to the Thessalonians. Peter's letters abound in it. And the book of Revelation is the greatest apocalypse ever written.

Now the sad thing about the use of apocalyptic literature in the history of the church is that it was ignored so long as the church prospered. It came back into favor only with the rebirth of persecution. And when it came back it was without careful examination of its key! The result was that apocalypses, especially the books of Daniel and Revelation, got interpreted in many fanciful ways because men were reading as literal statement the enigmas of the persecuted. Though students have in late years turned to a sane study of apocalyptic symbols, these queer interpretations have become so popularized as to make many sensible people feel that there is nothing for them in such a book as Revelation.

Practically all writings of this class employ the same kinds of symbols. They use numbers, such as 3 to symbolize the spirit world, 4 for the earth, 6 for humankind, 7 for the divine or the perfect, 12 for the church; the multiples and squares and cubes of these numbers being also found. They use colors: white for victory, red for strife, black for famine, greenish-gray (translated "pale") for death, and a number of others. They use heavenly bodies: blackened or eclipsed sun, bloody moon, falling stars, all as symbols of judgment that occur again and again upon the earth. They use beasts and monsters: the lion as symbolic of strength, the bear of stealth, the lamb of sacrifice. They use time symbols and many others. None of these should be taken literally. They were never meant to be so taken. Thus, when Daniel speaks of his famous "seventy weeks," or Revelation of its "thousand years," these are not really periods of time at all, only time symbols of great spiritual truths, seventy and one thousand being numbers of completeness. When Jesus speaks of the coming of the Son of man as being attended by the darkening of the sun, by the failing of the light of the moon, and by the falling of the stars from the sky, he is not predicting particular events, but employing the common literary language of his day in its figures of judgment and doom. When the book of Revelation says that the mystic number was "the number of a man," and then solemnly pronounces that number to be 666, the point is not to try to find a man in history whose name, evaluated in letters according to the dictionary, will work out to 666. There have been countless men whose names can be manipulated to this end. But the point is that the number of a *man*, without God's aid, is always a succession of sixes, the human number that falls one short of seven which is the perfect number of God.

The upshot of these comments on apocalyptic literature is this, that of all books of the Bible where the reader ought not to feel free to go ahead without intelligent note and comment, books like Daniel and Revelation are the chief. Until he can secure some good commentary that will explain their symbols he may treat them with but little attention. But when he does read them with good help he will find, especially in Revelation and in the apocalypse of Jesus (Matt., ch. 24, Mark, ch. 13, etc.), a wonderful faith expressed in hours of gloom, an interpretation of the religious life that is deep and true, even though it is not the only way to look at the truth.

Biblical Gospel

A unique contribution of our New Testament to world literature is the Gospel form. Matthew, Mark, Luke, and John are not, as we have seen, biographies in the modern sense of that term. They are as truly interpretations of the ministry of Jesus Christ as the writings of the prophets were of events in Israel's life. The Gospels, like the books of the prophets, deal with history, but are more than history. They might be called "suprahistorical"; that is, they make use of historical narrative, but put the kind of meaning into it that makes of it the proclamation of a message. Each Gospel is a series of historical events turned into a sermon.

Biblical Epistle

It remains to say a word about the kind of literature known as epistle. There are a few brief examples contained in books of the

Old Testament, but in the New this type of literature accounts for twenty-one of the twenty-seven books. An epistle is always a letter, yet it is nearly always something more than a letter, though the Revised Standard Version is satisfied to call each "epistle" a "letter." The epistle has more formality, less of the casual and temporary. Often it embodies a treatise on some subject, as is especially the case with Romans and Hebrews, yet a treatise that is so taken up in the atmosphere of correspondence that it is never dry or theoretical. The epistle thus is a definite form of literature, with its own qualities of style. It enables a writer to deal with questions of lasting moment, of interest beyond the occasion that gave rise to them, and yet do it in such a lively way as to ensure reading. A few of the epistles were probably written with the definite purpose of wide circulation. Others seem to show that their authors were unconsciously thinking beyond the bounds of their parochial lives. As in the case of the prophets and psalmists, it is not only pious, but also true, to say that the Holy Spirit used the minds and hearts of the writers of the New Testament epistles for larger ends than those writers themselves ever knew.

Chapter 12

THE CHALLENGE OF THE BIBLE

"If you know these things, blessed are you if you do them" (John 13: 17). So spoke the Master of men to his disciples. It is one thing to have information at hand; it is another to follow that information's lead. The old Greek idea that men who knew what was right would be strong and free stumbles before the realization of the amazing number who know and do not do.

> "Stand by the roads, and look,
>   and ask for the ancient paths,
>   where the good way is; and walk in it,
>   and find rest for your souls." (Jer. 6: 16)

It would seem that Jeremiah had done his duty when he got the people to inquire for the good way until they found it; but the prophet understood the human heart well enough to know that he needed to add the injunction, "walk in it." Tools and techniques can be laid before us in such completeness that we cannot escape them, but no power can force us to use them. Yet there may be incentives to action, and when these are great and varied there is much hope. The wonderful principles that comprise the Sermon on the Mount find their completion in the little parable at its close (Matt. 7: 24–27). Here Jesus challenges all who hear to submit their characters to the test of deeds. If they hear and do nothing they are like a house built on shifting sand; if they hear and do, their lives are as firmly founded as a house on a rock.

176

THE CHALLENGE OF THE BIBLE'S UNITY

In the matter of Bible reading, the challenge to act is as real as the knowledge of the way. There is, for one thing, the Bible's unity. We have been emphasizing the fact that in one sense each of its sixty-six books contains a unique message. Yet it is not mere romanticism that has pictured the Bible in terms of a living unity. It may leave a sense of the artificial to trace certain "golden threads" through the scriptures, and former generations may have so over-done the idea of harmony as to make us shy of seeing similarity in purpose and thought. But for all that, the bringing of this library of books together under one cover was no forced procedure. It was natural and, indeed, inevitable.

The best evidence for this lies in a study of the way in which the Bible as one volume came to be. In the Bibliography are suggestions for reading the fascinating story of the formation of the "canon" of the Bible, that is, the lists of books as we have them now. For there were other religious documents written both in the days of our Old Testament and in those of our New. It was the church that had to decide—the Jewish church in the one case, and the Christian church in the other—which of these documents to leave out and which to include in making up its Bible. We have every reason to believe that the church was guided by the Spirit of God in the mak-ing of a choice of those books which would best represent the mind of God for his children. And perhaps the best reason of all for believing that lies in the utter freedom from artificial compulsion that characterized the formation of the Old and New Testament canons.

These canons were both gradual growths. They were not brought into being by any arbitrary fiat. Neither voice from the sky nor requirement from church council was the origin of the choice. At first the Jewish Bible probably consisted only of the works attributed to Moses. The collection of the prophets certainly was not made in anything like complete form until well after the return from exile, while the poetical and other books experienced varied usage as late as the time of Christ, the Jews not finally deciding that such books as Daniel and the Song of Songs belonged in the Bible until nearly A.D. 100.

Similarly with our New Testament: the early Christian church did not say, "Now there are many gospel narratives of Jesus' life being written; therefore we must lay down the law as to which of them Christians shall use." Rather they gave attention to the work of spreading the kingdom, and let Christian reading grow by gradual recognition of what was true and worthy. One of our own Gospels testifies to the fact that many had taken in hand the task of recording what Jesus did and taught and what Christians believed (Luke 1: 1–4). But before any of the writing down, there was circulation by word of mouth of many of the stories about Jesus, especially of the week of his passion. As the firsthand witnesses of his ministry died and new generations of Christians arose, the believing communities felt the need of drawing up some account of the grounds of their belief. In some localities narratives of Jesus' activity were written; in others lists of his remembered sayings were prepared, often for the purpose of giving new converts teachings of the Master to study and memorize. Again there would be interpretation of acts of Jesus in terms of the worship which the church had come to pay to him. Gradually these various separate documents were brought together into a few larger accounts that we know as Gospels. By degrees, some that proved unworthy fell out of use, while the four that we now have became the common property of the church at large. But the test of their genuineness was their use, the growing feeling that these and these alone were the work of the Spirit. Even the first of the ecumenical councils of the church gave no attention to the canon of Scripture, and it was not until the latter part of the fourth century that a church council decreed what books were to be counted in the New Testament. Even then the decision was made on the basis of what was the most common practice among the churches.

If someone imagines that such a procedure must have led to a wide variety of usage among Christians, let him read history and

be amazed at the astonishing unity of the churches in the books
which they recognized without compulsion. Thus our four Gospels,
and no others among the many that were written, were recognized
by most of the churches as early as the middle of the second century,
while in the last quarter of the same century one of the great leaders
of the church could write that everywhere, except among a few of
the sects, there was universal agreement on the use of twenty books
for Christians. These twenty were our four Gospels, the book of
Acts (though several other Acts were written), thirteen letters of
Paul (just as we have them now), I Peter, and I John. That twenty
of our twenty-seven New Testament books should have been recognized and used by the church universal within seventy-five years
of the death of the last of the apostles is nothing short of marvelous.
In itself it constitutes a great challenge to the reading of church
people of today. And inasmuch as the Christian church adopted
bodily the Old Testament of the Hebrews, there was further unity
evident.

After all, why should this not be so? Varied as are the themes
and the viewpoints of the authors of these books, there is in practically all of them the insistence on monotheism; on the righteous
and loving nature of God as one and not as two opposing qualities;
on the helplessness of mankind in sin, a sin that constitutes a racial
unity of all classes and colors whether men will or no; on the graciousness of God in providing for men's overcoming of the blight of
sin; on the possibility of securing God's righteousness for men's
lives and the power for it in Christ; on the spiritual conception of
death and resurrection; and on the certainty of the triumph of the
kingdom of God. These books speak as one.

THE CHALLENGE OF USE

Yet when one turns the pages of the history of the church he is
saddened again and again by the foolish, selfish, thoughtless, and
even inhuman uses to which the Bible has been put. It would be
unbelievable, were not the evidence so overwhelming, the way in

which Christians have made the Bible a tool for superstition, a source of fear for men whom they would oppress, a stamping ground for little ideas taken from any larger setting and magnified out of all importance, and especially a kind of rope for use in a sordid tug of war, by which one Christian group may seek to pull another into a deep hole of some river of controversy.

It is not enough to have freed the Bible from the fetters of the Middle Ages and to have secured the right to read it for ourselves. We must read it in such a way and with such an object in view as to free it from the tighter fetters of our modern provincialisms and sectarianisms.

We need to avoid "bibliolatry." To worship the book as a book is but to practice another form of idolatry. We are saved by God in Christ, not by a book. The Bible is not a talisman, to be kept on some end table in the living room as a protection against the goblins of the soul. The black binding, gilt edges, and limp leather in which many of our Bibles come, the phrase "Holy Bible" awesomely printed on the cover, the reverence in which it is rightfully used, all these can become but the means of defeating its real purpose. To use it as a dynamic for life is the only cure for this sin.

We err also when we use it to "prove" something that we want to establish in controversy. Most of the time we do not prove anything at all, and even where we do, our spirit in using it is wrong. The Bible is not an arsenal of argument, not a boon to our pet theories. It is to be used for binding people together, not for driving them apart. Wherever it has been the source of opposing schools of theology, of sectarian split, of unbalanced proclamation of some smaller truth, there it has been used only partially and there it has been interpreted wrongfully, not alone by one of the parties concerned, but generally by both. "Thy word is a lamp," but never a destroying fire. The Bible is a weapon, yet not of defense for self, but of offense for living against the evil of the world, the "sword of the Spirit."

And above all we need so to read and use our Bibles as to end the hiatus that has long existed between personal piety and greed in social relations. One of the gravest single counts against Protestant Christianity in America is the number of people it has produced who are sincere, devout Christians in what we frequently think of as the private relations of life, but beasts of prey when they get out on the marts of trade or strive to rise in the social scheme. This has resulted from using the Bible as a source of comfort only, of personal reflection and enjoyment, of intake instead of inspiration for outgo. While the Bible admittedly contains no panacea for social ills, it altogether misses its mark with any given Christian unless it inspires that person to seek the will of God in all relations and to bear daily the cross of the denial of self in the race of life. All else is selfish use of the sourcebook of unselfish religion, a trying to find the road to heaven for oneself while blocking off the road to abundant life for one's fellows.

EACH CHRISTIAN HAS HIS OWN BIBLE

We need also to realize that belief in the Bible does not consist in verbal admission that sixty-six books belong to an inspired canon. Each Christian has a canon of his own. It consists of the books he actually reads again and again, knows truly, and seeks to live by. There are some of the best books of the Bible that the average Christian knows nothing of. To neglect is to deny. How large is my canon? Twelve books out of the sixty-six? Twenty? And if I have read them all, and feel I know pretty well the contents of each, how much real influence does any given one have on the life I live? This is the final test of canonicity. Only in so far as we all come to a unity of faith and life can we find a oneness of religion that is actually based on the Bible. Then alone shall we realize the truth of the daring claim of the apostle, "All scripture is inspired by God and profitable for teaching, for reproof, for correction, and for training in righteousness, that the man of God may be complete, equipped for every good work" (II Tim. 3: 16, 17).

The Ultimate Purpose in Reading the Bible

But it needs to be emphasized that the reading of the Bible is not an end in itself. One may read in prodigious quantities and with increasing frequency and be little the better spiritually. One may have developed even such a good habit as that of reading his Bible with a pencil, making all kinds of notes in the margin. He may go so far as to write out his own comments. He may memorize long passages as he reads—in itself the truest reading. Yet he may do it all as an accomplishment or even as a task. The mere knowing of the Bible, however thoroughly done, may not produce an effective life.

We are not transformed by knowledge of a book, but by fellowship with a Person. All of us are persons, and our lives are satisfactory only as they are adequately related to one who is the Complete Person. Abraham was called the friend of God. Moses knew God face to face. David was a man after God's own heart. Nearly eight centuries before the time of Christ, Hosea told the people of Israel that the knowledge of God was more important than even the trappings of worship (Hos. 6: 6). The Bible is simply the tool to that knowledge.

So also the insistence of Christianity on the person of Christ is for no mere dogmatic reasons. It is because in Jesus Christ the real nature of God is so completely revealed that the early church taught that there was salvation in no other name but his (Acts 4: 12). Paul again and again urges his readers to attain fellowship in Christ, for in so doing they would really come to know and love and obey God. The Bible, especially the New Testament, fulfills its purpose by introducing us adequately to God in Christ. Unless we learn to know him and fellowship with him, reading the Bible is fruitless. Life in its richest meaning is the issue of such a fellowship. "And this is eternal life, that they know thee the only true God, and Jesus Christ whom thou has sent" (John 17:3).

A SELECTED BIBLIOGRAPHY

Those who wish to devote more time to their reading and study of the Bible will find help in the following books.

TRANSLATIONS OF THE BIBLE

The King James Bible. Often called "The Authorized Bible."
> The classic English version, published in 1611, of inestimable influence on our language, thought, and life.
> Available in many editions.

The Revised Standard Version. New York, Thomas Nelson & Sons, 1946, 1952.
> The most accurate and attractive English text of today.

Moulton, R. G. (editor), *The Modern Reader's Bible*. New York, The Macmillan Co., 1895.
> Makes use of the text of the English Revised Version of 1881, but has a very attractive and suggestive arrangement of the books of the Bible according to their literary forms.

Weymouth, R. F., *The New Testament*. Boston, Pilgrim Press, Fifth Edition, 1929.
> Presently published, New York, Harper & Bros.

Moffatt, James, *The Holy Bible: A New Translation*. New York, Harper & Bros., 1935.
> Excellent on the New Testament, especially on the Epistles of Paul.
> Plays fast and loose with the Old Testament, both in text and arrangement of material.

183

Smith, J. M. P., and Goodspeed, E. J., *The Bible: An American Translation*. Chicago, University of Chicago Press, Rev. Ed., 1935.
The Old Testament translated under the editorship of Dr. Powis-Smith; the New Testament by Dr. Goodspeed.
Based on the belief that the Bible was written in the speech of ordinary men, this is an excellent effort to give Americans the Bible in dignified spoken American English. Especially good on the Gospels.

Phillips, J. B., *The Gospels*. New York, The Macmillan Co., 1953.
All the Phillips' translations of the New Testament are proving an inspiration to Bible reading because of their clear and up-to-date wording and their pungent style.

Phillips, J. B., *The Young Church in Action*. New York, The Macmillan Co., 1955.
A translation of the Book of Acts.

Phillips, J. B., *Letters to Young Churches*. New York, The Macmillan Co., 1948, 1957.
The first of the Phillips series and the one on which his reputation as a translator was built.

Phillips, J. B., *The Book of Revelation*. New York, The Macmillan Co., 1957.
This translation by Phillips is based on the conviction that Revelation is a mystery and that therefore the translation ought to preserve the atmosphere of mystery.

Phillips, J. B., *The New Testament in Modern English*. New York, The Macmillan Co., 1958.
The foregoing four volumes in one.

Bible Stories for Children

Faris, J. T., *Standard Bible Story Readers: Books I–VI*. New York, Platt-Munk Co.
The first three volumes are especially attractive for young children; they are full of pictures, with a few big words on the page, as the child of 3–6 delights to find his books.

Sherman, Henry A., and Kent, Charles F., *The Children's Bible*. New York, Chas. Scribner's Sons, 1922.
Long tested and proved as most readable for children of 8–12. It is a beautifully illustrated telling of the stories of the Bible, including some of the epistles.

Bowie, W. R., *The Story of the Bible*. New York, Abingdon Press, 1934.

Paterson-Smythe, John, *A Boys' and Girls' Life of Christ*. New York, Revell, 1929.

Smither, E. L., *The Use of the Bible with Children*. New York, Abingdon Press, 1937.
Very suggestive.

Commentaries on the Bible

The Holy Bible: Westminster Study Edition. Philadelphia, Westminster Press, 1948.
Contains the text of the Bible in the King James Version, general introductory articles, special introductions to each book, and commentary.

Dummelow, J. R., *A Commentary on the Holy Bible*. New York, Macmillan, 1908, revised edition, 1930.
Similar in content to the Westminster edition except that it does not contain the text of the Bible itself.

Eiselen, F. C., Lewis, E., and Downey, D. G., *The Abingdon Bible Commentary*. New York, Abingdon Press, 1929.
Similar in content to Dummelow's.

Peake, A. S., *Commentary on the Bible*. New York, Thomas Nelson & Sons, 1919.

Daily Bible Studies. Philadelphia, Westminster Press, 1957, etc.
An American edition of the Scottish commentary on the New Testament for laymen, edited by William Barclay. Clear and fresh in style, well outlined, but detailed and rather British in background.

The Interpreter's Bible, Vols. I–XII. New York, Abingdon Press, 1951.
Contains the text of the Bible in both King James and Revised Standard Version, with articles of general and special introduction, scholarly exegesis and popular exposition of each book. Quite elaborate, but used by some laymen.

Erdman, C., *Commentaries on New Testament Books*. Philadelphia, Westminster Press.
Devotional and readable.

Torch Bible Commentaries. New York, The Macmillan Co.

Books on the Reading and Study of the Bible

Rowley, H. H., *The Unity of the Bible*. London, Carey Kingsgate, 1953.
For those who have already read considerably in books about the
Bible.

Richardson, Alan, *A Preface to Bible Study*. Philadelphia, Westminster
Press, 1944.
An excellent brief introduction to Bible study.

Anderson, Bernhard W., *Rediscovering the Bible*. New York, Association Press, 1951.
Rather general, but helpful.

Anderson, Bernhard W., *The Unfolding Drama of the Bible*. New
York, Association Press, 1957.

Ferguson, Walter Dewey, *Journey Through the Bible*. New York,
Harper & Bros., 1947.
Simple and in story form.

Dodd, C. H., *The Bible Today*. New York, The Macmillan Co., 1947.
Brief, but illuminating.

Swaim, J. C., *Right and Wrong Ways to Use the Bible*. Philadelphia,
Westminster Press, 1953.

Swaim, J. C., *Do You Understand the Bible?* Philadelphia, Westminster
Press, 1954.
These books of Swaim's are full of suggestive illustrations.

Brown, Robert M., *The Bible Speaks to You*. Philadelphia, Westminster
Press, 1955.

Suggs, M. J., *The Layman Reads His Bible*. St. Louis, Bethany Press,
1957.

Books on the Two Testaments

Francisco, A., *Introducing the Old Testament*. Nashville, Broadman
Press, 1950.
The most readable general introduction to the Old Testament.

Anderson, Bernhard W., *Understanding the Old Testament*. Englewood Cliffs, N.J., Prentice Hall, 1957.
Contains a wealth of background material.

Sloan, J. R., *A Survey of the Old Testament*. New York, Abingdon
Press, 1957.
Gives attention to each book.

Filson, F. V., *Opening the New Testament*. Philadelphia, Westminster Press, 1952.
> The best brief introduction to the New Testament in general and each book in particular. Goes well with Francisco's book on the Old Testament.

Kee, H. C., and Young, F. W., *Understanding the New Testament*. Englewood Cliffs, N.J., Prentice Hall, 1957.
> A companion book to Anderson's on the Old Testament.

Hunter, A. M., *The Message of the New Testament*. Philadelphia, Westminster Press, 1944.
> Brief, but shows clearly the unity of the New Testament theme.

Fraser, I. W., *Understanding the New Testament*. New York, Abingdon Press, 1946.

Bright, John, *The Kingdom of God*. New York, Abingdon Press, 1953.
> The best book for seeing the unity of the two Testaments under a single theme.

Books on Parts of the Bible

Kirkpatrick, A. F., *The Psalms*, in Cambridge Bible Series, 2 Vols. New York, Cambridge University Press.
> Devout, scholarly, and quite readable.

Leslie, E. A., *The Psalms*. New York, Abingdon Press, 1949.
> Represents a point of view new to many. Interesting and readable.

Scott, R. B. Y., *The Relevance of the Prophets*. New York, The Macmillan Co., 1944.
> A good understandable discussion of the prophets and the meaning of their message for today.

Paterson, John, *The Goodly Fellowship of the Prophets*. New York, Chas. Scribner's Sons, 1953. A good systematic treatment.

Love, Julian Price, *The Gospel and the Gospels*. New York, Abingdon Press, 1953.
> An attempt to use the results of careful scholarship to develop from their various portions the messages of the Gospels.

Dodd, C. H., *The Parables of the Kingdom*. New York, Chas. Scribner's Sons, 1936.
> Scholarly but readable.

Poteat, E. M., *Parables of Crisis*. New York, Harper & Bros., 1950.
> Reads like good story sermons.

Stalker, James, *Life of Christ*. New York, Revell, 1909.
Old, but simple and clear.

Smith, David, *The Days of His Flesh*. New York, Harper & Bros.
Follows the Gospels closely and in some detail.

Taylor, Vincent, *The Life and Ministry of Jesus*. New York, Abingdon Press, 1955.
For more advanced readers.

Stewart, James S., *The Life and Teachings of Jesus Christ*. Richmond, John Knox Press, 1933.
An excellent combination of a life of Christ and interpretation of his significance to humanity.

Stewart, James S., *A Man in Christ*. London, Hodder & Stoughton, 1938.
A very appreciative and well written life of Paul.

Miller, D. G., *Conqueror in Chains*. Philadelphia, Westminster Press, 1951.
A delightful life of Paul for young people.

Quimby, C. W., *Paul for Everyone*. New York, The Macmillan Co., 1944.
Intended for laymen.

Robinson, *The Life of Paul*. Chicago, University of Chicago Press, revised edition, 1934.
Clear, and especially good in relating Paul's letters to his travels.

Smith, David, *The Life and Letters of Paul*. New York, Harper & Bros.
A companion to the author's *The Days of His Flesh*.

Coneybeare, W. J., and Howson, J. S., *The Life and Letters of St. Paul*. Grand Rapids, Eerdman's Co., 1951.

Harmonies of the Gospels

Stevens, William Arnold, and Burton, Ernest De Witt, *A Harmony of the Gospels for Historical Study*. Boston, Silver Burdett & Company, 1896.
Old, but valuable in attempt to arrange in chronological order the material of all four Gospels.

Burton, Ernest De Witt, and Goodspeed, Edgar Johnson, *A Harmony of the Synoptic Gospels*. New York, Chas. Scribner's Sons, 1917.
More scientific than the foregoing, but omits the Gospel of John.

Bundy, Walter Ernest, A Syllabus and Synopsis of the First Three
    Gospels. Indianapolis, The Bobbs-Merrill Co.
    An excellent arrangement and interrelation of the texts of the first
    three Gospels.
Gospel Parallels. New York, Thomas Nelson and Sons, 1949.
    Makes use of the Revised Standard Version in its harmony of the
    first three Gospels.

The Making of the Bible

Bruce, F. F., The Books and the Parchments. London, Pickering and
    Inglis, 1953.
Filson, F. V., Which Books Belong in the Bible? Philadelphia, West-
    minster Press, 1957.
    A clearly written justification of the Protestant canon of scripture.
May, W. J., Our English Bible in the Making. Philadelphia, West-
    minster Press, 1952.
    The most satisfactory book on the history of our English Bible.
Smyth, John Paterson, How We Got Our Bible. New York, Harper &
    Bros., 1899.
    Old, and not up to date in several respects, but very interesting.

Bible Times

Heaton, Eric W., Everyday Life in Old Testament Times. New York,
    Chas. Scribner's Sons, 1956.
Bouquet, Alan Coates, Everyday Life in New Testament Times. New
    York, Chas. Scribner's Sons, 1954.

Biblical Tools

Davis, J. D., and Gehman, H. S., The Westminster Dictionary of the
    Bible. Philadelphia, Westminster Press, revised edition, 1944.
    The best one volume Bible dictionary for the layman.
Wright, G. E., and Filson, F. V., The Westminster Historical Atlas to
    the Bible. Philadelphia, Westminster Press, 1945.
Young, Robert, Analytical Concordance. New York, Funk and Wagnalls,
    1893.
    Old, but very useful.